04

T0053751

Edited by Isabel Lewis,
Adrea Piazza, Andrea Sandell
Distributed by Harvard University Press
London, England, and Cambridge, Massachusetts

For its fourth issue, *Pairs* was asked to stand on its own. The editors who brought *Pairs 01* to life in 2020 in the midst of the COVID-19 pandemic have by now all graduated from the Harvard Graduate School of Design, leaving behind a journal grounded in the spirit of conversation. In fact, it is because of its very format, one in which we—the students—engage in conversation around "objects" with others, that this journal so swiftly became a self-sustaining project, able to be passed on to each subsequent generation of classmates.

    Pairs provides a rare opportunity to create a physical record of the ideas and interests that are both blatantly and subterraneously circulating in our school. These ideas are distilled not a priori, through a thematic call-and-response, but rather through a slow, collaborative process of sharing and discussing. Over the past year, the editors and contributors of *Pairs 04* learned from each other about emerging voices and the criticisms of past voices, they uncovered forgotten objects and hidden histories, and they reminded each other to look beyond what is expected.

    These multidisciplinary exchanges should not be misinterpreted as a byproduct of more fluid and hyphenate modes of design. While the curiosity to look beyond the confines of our own disciplines drives many of the conversations present in this issue, questions of how we practice are inextricably linked to the often forgotten questions of who we practice for. The labor of design, its publics and users, and the limits and potentials of our agency as young practitioners serendipitously emerged in many of the conversations that follow.

    Thus, if *Pairs* is a publication by students, it is even more a publication for students. It is produced through attentive labor and care, brought together by the spirit to share with each other new topics for conversation. Of course, despite our best efforts, each pairing comes with its own constraints. The labor offered by each of our contributors is genuine, and it is our continued hope that the Harvard GSD administration will recognize the *Pairs* team as workers. Our greatest concern is that access to the already limited project of *Pairs* becomes further constrained; this journal can only fail if it no longer represents the student body. Despite these challenges, or perhaps because of them, we hope that the spirit of this journal—one centered on curiosity, criticism, and conversation—continues to thrive independently among our audience. By, for, and from students. That is, after all, how this publication started.

The team that brought *Pairs 04* to life is the largest one yet, comprising 15 students who represent, for the first time, all master's degree programs housed at the Harvard GSD. Student contributors in this issue posed questions about labor, provenance, ecology, justice, and memory. We spoke with a journalist about the steel industry and hyperpop, with a geographer about early computer maps and the scourge of landlords, with an archaeologist about decay, and with a curator about mermaids. Of course, a number of designers joined us as well: they span five decades in age and work across various scales and on different continents. Through this diversity, we are reminded how conversations about design can exceed the assumed boundaries of our respective disciplines. It is precisely through design thinking in its most versatile form that we can engage with topics that might seem far removed from our own professions but in reality hold the potential to critcally examine them.

Isabel, Adrea, and Andrea

LETTER FROM THE EDITORS

Emily Wettstein & MLA Welcome Package

Sophie Weston Chien & Emily Wettstein

SOPHIE WESTON CHIEN

I first saw the Master in Landscape Architecture (MLA) welcome packages on Instagram during COVID, when I was a prospective student after finishing my undergraduate thesis.[1] I was drawn

MLA welcome packages were kits that included laser-cut parts for students' first studio site model, large plots and prints, scale people cards, isometric and dot notepads, AutoCAD lineweight cheat-sheets, an elm tree leaf from Harvard Yard, and a handwritten note. When the GSD was completely remote in 2020, the kits were organized by Emily Wettstein and mailed to 37 incoming MLA students.

to them because they broke the Zoom wall for me. Here was an educator who was trying to meaningfully connect the physical world with an online curriculum. What started the welcome package idea? What were the circumstances like for you and your students?

EMILY WETTSTEIN

Let's think back to this moment. Students were about to start their semester virtually, and my TAs and I were collaborating on how to make them feel welcome and grounded in their first semester. We thought about how meaningful it is to be embodied in a space with other people and how hard that might be because that was not possible during COVID. We started to brainstorm things that we could share with them. Then my TA, Melissa Eloshway, thought about how students normally get their desks the first day, with kits filled with different materials for preterm workshop. How could we share that spirit? There's something about getting your desk that's like getting a place in this little world. So, how can we do that? From the beginning, it was about a deep moment of care and personal connection.

SWC

It's a great way to frame what a student needs to begin the semester and to set the groundwork for coming together as a cohort. Connection is also a necessary ingredient in establishing relationships between teachers and students.

EW

Yes, and also among students. I was surprised to find out how much the students felt the kits connected them, the fact that they shared this common thing. It was a conversation starter, but also it felt like they were all starting from the same point. It was not really about the logistics but actually the interrelationships among us as a community.

SWC

Reading some of the feedback that you received from students about the welcome package, I was struck by the impact it had on how students felt. It gave them proof that they were starting school, and it made them feel like they were welcomed into a community.[2] There was also an access component to it, ensuring

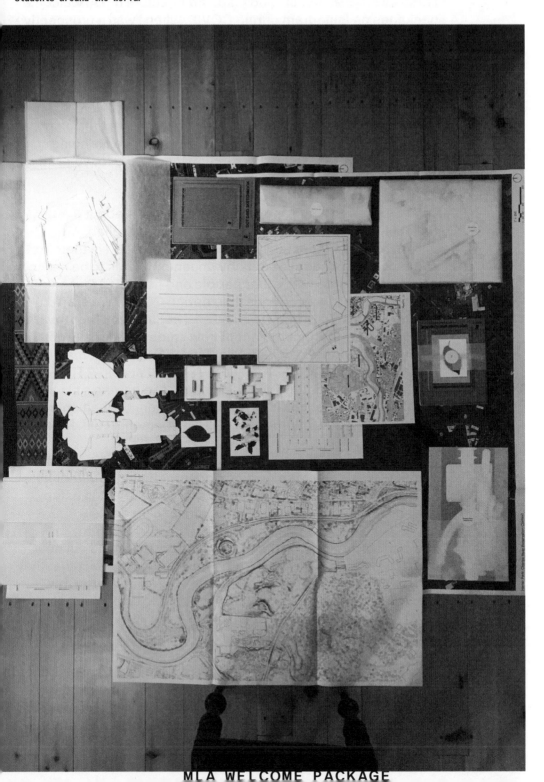

fig. 1 MLA welcome packages in-process before being shipped from Emily's living room to incoming students around the world.

MLA WELCOME PACKAGE

One testimonial: "Emily's handwritten card was so sweet! And the American elm leaf enclosed to connect us to Harvard Yard was a really thoughtful token that also felt specific to the landscape architecture program. And you've got to love a keychain measuring tape."

all students had the exact same materials and parity as they entered the program. How have you reincorporated those values into in-person teaching?

EW

Something that I realized reading those responses is how important the threshold of beginning education is. It's a make-or-break instant and sets the tone for everything after. It's a really pivotal inclusion moment.

SWC

The orientation leader in me loves a good ceremony to kick things off.

EW

There is something a little bit performative about the box, too.

SWC

For sure.

EW

Specifically, we included welcome notes that were really per-sonal and warm, and they dissolved the separation between student and instructor. That extreme hierarchy needs to break down in general.

SWC

To that point, the impact of the packages on the students after they knew that you handwrote the notes, I think, disrupted labor relations. Student–teacher relationships can mimic an office dynamic of manager and employee. Instead, you began teaching by laboring for your class, which I'm sure set the tone for creat-ing a different relationship between student and teacher.

EW

Yeah, and I was also really determined to handwrite each note, even though my handwriting is terrible.

SWC

Transitioning from the MLA welcome packages to the broader context of design education, what do you think the role of care is in pedagogy? I think about teaching from a place of emergence, where there is no linear process or single correct method. This involves meeting students where they are and learning what they are interested in. It requires teachers to accept a diversity of work and relax control over what a student designs. In many ways, care requires design education to slow down and prioritize students' self-actualization alongside their development of technical skills. How do you care for your students, why is care important and novel, and what do your pedagogical methods look like?

EW

The reality is that we are weeding students out in our pedagogy, but we're selecting for the wrong qualities. There is the survival of the fittest in every studio program. But we need to take a look at the students and the qualities that we're losing, which are incredible attributes, because we're sticking to a "tough love" pedagogical model. At the end of the day, are we weeding out sensitivity? Are we weeding out true, deep empathy?

When I started to teach right after finishing grad school, the experience of being a student was so fresh to me. I felt so aware of the privilege of teaching, and I knew it couldn't just be about reaching the few students that my teaching resonated with the most. There were many other students who weren't being reached. There needs to be more care to bring all students into the pedagogy and to realize how much emotions affect our learning.

Those were my instincts when I started to teach, and I was encouraged to shut those down because traditional pedagogy doesn't take care of students. I'm still frustrated ... why do we have to teach like this? Women worked so hard to get in these positions—do we have to now play by the same oppressive rules? We're at a stage where we no longer should just feel thankful to be here and shape these institutions to work better instead.

SWC

In line with this conversation on care is a theory you've developed called Student As Site, which is an approach from landscape architecture that I think should be applied to design education at large. Can you describe what it is and how you developed it?

EW

As a concurrent dual-degree student at the GSD, I was doing this back-and-forth between architecture and landscape architecture, and it made me hyperaware of the differences between the disciplines. The most salient difference was how each discipline approached site. The discipline of landscape architecture approaches site design by acknowledging that the site is thick and complex and has ongoing processes and histories and layers. That sensitivity was largely ignored in architecture, where the site is much more about the object. In landscape architecture, the latent qualities of the site are the basis for the design process.

However, in design school there is a "clean slate" approach to students themselves: go back to page zero, forget, unlearn everything you knew before. But those are actually the reasons

fig. 2 Diagram of MLA welcome package components and their stacked arrangement. Handwritten notes were placed near the top, beneath a sheet of scale figures.

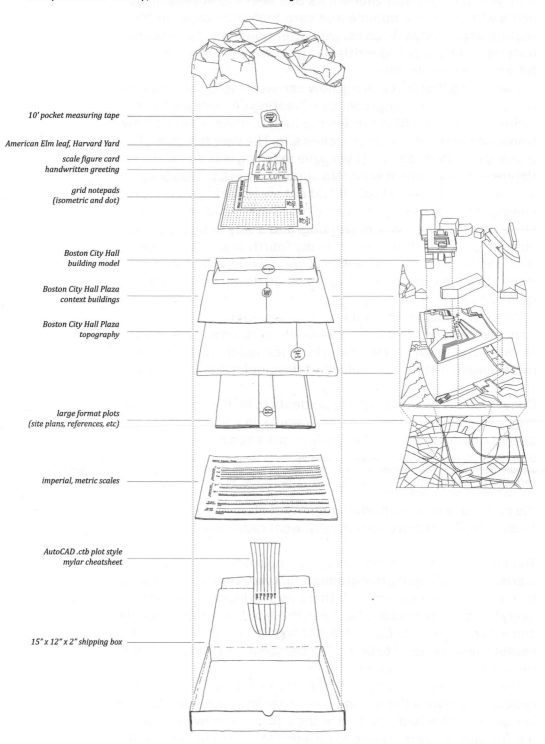

10' pocket measuring tape

American Elm leaf, Harvard Yard

scale figure card
handwritten greeting

grid notepads
(isometric and dot)

Boston City Hall
building model

Boston City Hall Plaza
context buildings

Boston City Hall Plaza
topography

large format plots
(site plans, references, etc)

imperial, metric scales

AutoCAD .ctb plot style
mylar cheatsheet

15" x 12" x 2" shipping box

we want people here! How can we build your design practice from your background? Student As Site seeks to approach students with the same nuance and care that landscape architecture approaches its sites: with attention to processes and histories and layered identities as generative of their own futures and complexities.

Translating that to teaching, how can we develop our students through those same approaches? Creating our own mode of inclusivity and teaching tactics, we look to sitedness and how landscape in particular approaches site. The very first line of the very first exercise that I ever gave teaching was in "Landscape Representation," and it was: "No student enters the GSD as a clean slate." Looking back, it laid out my teaching philosophy moving forward. A lot of that came from having had an artistic life, a creative life, a way of working, and a way of being before starting the GSD. It took me until my fourth year in a five-year dual-degree program to develop a way of working that incorporated all of the ways of working that I had developed prior to grad school.

When that finally clicked, it was incredible. It was a totally transformative experience when I was finally working in a way that resonated with who I was. When I started teaching, I needed to make sure that students could start developing that sense early.

SWC

Conversations around teaching students to be their whole selves are becoming more common, for example, in the work that I do as part of Dark Matter U.[3] Yet, they're still seen as separate from

Dark Matter U is a democratic network guided by the principle that we cannot survive and thrive without immediate change toward anti-racist models of design education and practice. Founded in 2020, Dark Matter U works inside and outside of existing systems to challenge, inform, and reorient our institutions toward a just future.

the pedagogy of design education. What shaped your approach to teaching? And more specifically, what radicalized you?

EW

The first thing that pushed me against normativity was when I started to teach right after graduating: I was very aware I had to be fully myself at that moment. There was no illusion that I knew everything. There couldn't be. I was there to learn with students, and we were going to figure it out together. I needed to be vulnerable, and I needed to be my full person if I was going to take this on. It was really daunting.

The first group of students that I ever taught at the GSD was radicalizing. During the second week of school, a student told me her grandmother had just died at the end of the previous semester. The student said: "I need to do a project about her land and her property and her life. I can tell that you're okay with the complexity and the fullness of me coming to this as a full person." To be a part of such a deeply moving and personal and important project to her but also what the project said about the discipline and about what landscape can do was very powerful.

The other radicalizing moment was spending an absolutely huge amount of time in office hours during my first semester teaching. I wanted to know the personal experience of each of my students, and so I spent 16 hours a week in office hours talking to students. That was a radicalizing experience because I understood who they were, what support they needed, what was working for them, and what wasn't working for them in this whole ecosystem. Those conversations built my sensitivity, awareness, and attention.

SWC

I'm very interested in teaching and have been talking to a lot of professors about their process of getting started. Most people have a difficult time sharing advice because there is no clear or direct path into design academia. I've been told that teaching starts out as very precarious. How has transitioning from student to critic to tenure-track professor been, and how have you experienced interpersonal or institutional care in the process?

EW

I spent so much time as a student caring for and being closely attuned to some of my classmates who were struggling in the system as it was. When I was put in the teaching position, it was like, okay, how do I reach the full spectrum of students? And further, how do I utilize the incredible insights that students have on teaching and learning? I want to shift how we frame pedagogy from a practice of teaching to a practice of teaching and learning. I'm interested in the pedagogy students design as students, giving agency to students to not just be reflective and projective but actually to be designers of what education can be.

It was important for me to chart my own way. I'm very grateful that my first teaching experience was not co-teaching. Because I wasn't with a more experienced teacher, I could teach in the way that I wished I had been taught and the way that I wished my classmates had been taught and not teach in the way that teaching had always happened. I tried not to talk to many people about my teaching when I started because I found that the advice I was being given didn't resonate with who I really was. A big thing for me was feeling like I was supposed to know how all of this worked and that I was supposed to know how to climb the teaching ladder. I mean, I just felt a lot of imposter syndrome.

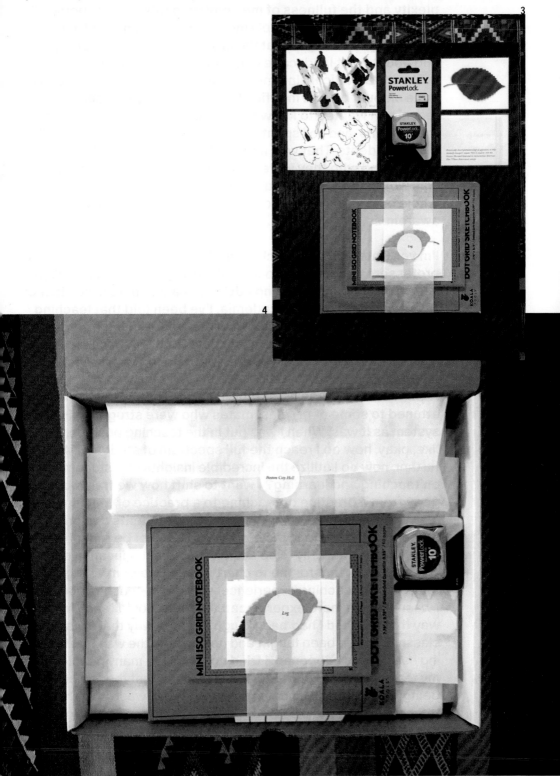

fig. 3 and *fig.* 4 MLA welcome package opened to reveal supplies and prepared materials.

MLA WELCOME PACKAGE

No one talks about how to start teaching. It's still one of these things—I'm an industry baby, and I have no idea how to get a teaching job or how to properly prepare for one.

EW

Right, yeah. Feeling a lot of imposter syndrome transitioning from being a student to being a professor, especially at the GSD, is very difficult. I couldn't fully take myself seriously in that space. For me, it has been important to step away from the GSD and begin teaching at a new school. Teaching felt like a mystery, and I felt like I was just very lucky to be there and couldn't really ask for clarity or push back on standard design teaching practices or the pedagogies I was inheriting.

SWC

So, who is taking care of you?

EW

I feel a real sense of care from my colleagues at UVA.[4] I feel very

Emily is currently an assistant professor of landscape architecture at the University of Virginia.

lucky, like we're on the same team and pushing toward something together. Jacob, my partner, takes care of me, and Lulu, my cat, and you, Sophie. I think there's been a transition in realizing that the work that I want to do is collaborative and that I can't keep trying to fit a round peg in a square hole. The work I do needs to be collaborative and it also needs to be with students. I've spent the last six years facilitating other people's creative processes and loving that because I'm part of them. But I've struggled with losing my own creative process. As I do this teaching thing, really fully do this thing, I need to get back in touch with my own process and not work against it. The biggest struggle for me is developing a sense of ownership and synthesizing my teaching process and my design process. I feel like when I can get a sense of that, that's going to feel really exciting and feel really good. This is not so dissimilar to the struggle in my graduate education of finding out in the fourth year that I could actually use all of my ways of working to find synergy. I'm looking for that: how research and teaching click and all of this becomes fluid. Teaching feels creative to me in many ways, but there's still something else that needs to be developed. Finding a way that research can feel intuitive and creative as well is something we're going to figure out together, Sophie.

SWC

What a great segue: the last thing I want to talk about is collectivity and new modes of research that intuitively reflect identity. We started our own collaborative called Seeding Pedagogies, about a year ago, after many conversations and frustrations with contemporary design education.[5] What are some ideas that you

Seeding Pedagogies Collaborative designs emergent landscape-forward pedagogies. In rejection of the status quo, the collective develops conditions for design students to thrive and facilitates pluralist forms of knowledge production.

want to work on through the collaborative?

SWC

EW

Seeding Pedagogies Collaborative is a group of people, a space, a process, a way of questioning inherited pedagogies and playing and experimenting with designing new ones. We speculate on futures untold or unseen and exercise the same design optimism that we deploy in studios but in our pedagogies as well. We focus on the way we teach, not just what we teach and the method, with the intent of being generative toward another future.

SWC

Let's dream for a bit. What are your long-term goals to change academia? What does the ethos of the welcome package scaled up to an entire school look like?

EW

The ethos scaled up to an entire school entails a real deep questioning and reckoning with the inherited practices of teaching and learning that we have taken on and figuring out what it means to teach totally differently.

SWC

My answer is always, I want my grandma to see herself as a designer even though she never went to design school. How do we reframe design education to be something that's not only for six credits at the end of a semester or for an accreditation or a professional license?

EW

Yeah, totally. And how is pedagogy deeply creative on all levels? I feel like we just demand our students to be creative in these certain very prescribed ways. But what does it mean for us to come back again to interrelationships and back to our connections and scale up from there in some way? Also I would love to know and to actualize at some point, what is a landscape? A questioning of what landscape is in a bigger and deeper sense of what it is, and then what its potentials are and then what are ... I don't know. This is a tough one, Sophie.

SWC

I think you're taking on the design of a school as a project like you took on the welcome package as a design project itself.

EW

Right.

SWC

School systems are inherited. All of these things are inherited for very specific reasons. Maybe we don't start from scratch, but we start from the site we are at now. How do we design from that?

EW

That's right. Something that I hope for Seeding Pedagogies is to bring pedagogy into a design language that we understand. And what is a pedagogy in which a true and genuine diversity of students can thrive and can collaborate and be part of something bigger than themselves? How we can model different futures is a big project.

Danielle Aubert & Harvard University Strike Posters

Audrey Watkins & Danielle Aubert

fig. 1 Poster from the 1969 student strike at Harvard University.

AUDREY WATKINS

I want to refresh our understanding of the events that took place at Harvard in 1969. Following the nationally covered occupations and protests at Columbia, Berkeley, and many other universities, the Harvard chapter of the Students for a Democratic Society (SDS) planned an occupation of University Hall to protest Harvard's Reserve Officer Training Corps (ROTC) program.[1]

The Students for a Democratic Society was a student organization with chapters on many college campuses in the 1960s. Active at Berkeley and partially responsible for the shutdown at Columbia in 1968, the group supported leftist culture and actions throughout the United States.

The occupation started with 70 students, a number that quickly grew to nearly 500. The university responded by sending 400 police officers to remove the students from University Hall, which sparked broader campus involvement. Classes shut down. This was when the strike posters came into play: an ad hoc print shop staffed by students—from the Harvard Graduate School of Design and the Massachusetts Institute of Technology—opened in the basement of University Hall, producing the posters we now find in the Harvard University Strike Posters Collection. A few days into the shutdown, an enormous public meeting was held at Harvard Stadium, and students voted to continue the strike, which went on for another week.

Harvard ultimately broke ties with the ROTC program and, with student involvement, formalized the African American Studies Department. For many students, this protest was their first experience with activist organizing. The strikes of 1969 were well before your time, but you have a background in labor organizing and design for collective action. What were your first experiences in those areas?

DANIELLE AUBERT

My first experience was the Yale strike. I was a grad student at Yale from 2002 to 2005. The four unions at Yale went on strike at the same time. It was huge. Getting all those unions to strike together required a certain level of organization. People were flying in for the strike, Cornel West was there, presidential candidates were there, and they shut down parts of New Haven. It was a powerful moment. At the time, I was new to the Graduate Employees Organizing Committee (GEOC), and we were trying to organize the grad student union.[2] I started to design some

The union UNITE HERE Local 33 was recognized in January 2023.

things very unofficially. For a rally around student debt, we made simple signs where students wrote how much debt they owed to Yale and put it on their backs.

Such a good idea. I could see myself doing that.

That was one of my first real actions. Around the same time Paul Elliman, a designer from the UK, was doing a workshop at Yale, and he had people make signs related to the Iraq War protests. We had an impeach Bush sign that said "Imp Each Bush," because at that time we had George W. Bush in office and had been through George H.W. Bush's presidency.

Were there specific design choices going into those actions and slogans?

A lot of the academic projects I was doing at the time were really worked over and detail-oriented. I made the protest posters really fast. They were so simple, just text. They're not acts of genius. I was trying to channel what someone wants to see in a crowd and what will create a mood or feeling of power. Sometimes you can be timid about your politics and about what you're willing to say in a group, but you have to go hard in a protest.

What are your first impressions of the posters from the 1969 strike? What stood out to you?

Well, I really like this one, "Strike for the Eight Demands." It's handwritten, but it's also a long list. I like the long list. The formal decisions look like they're made for speed. The type is obviously done by hand because the *A*s don't have crossbars, which would make it easier to cut for screen printing. They might have just been cutting out pieces of paper and sticking them directly on the screen.

The poster that reads, "Lesson 1, Conjugation for Subjugation," reminds me of a French May 68 poster that says, "*je participe, tu participes, il participe, nous participons, vous participez, ils profitent,*" which basically translates to "we participate and they profit."[3] Also this typeface is cool, with this ligature between the

In May 1968, parallel to events happening in the US, strikes broke out across France in response to capitalist social trends as well as to rebuke traditionalism.

S and the *T.*

It's funny that the students are at school and framing the poster as a lesson. When you design a protest poster, how do you balance the message and the amount of information to include? If you imagine creating an informational scheme for a cause,

fig. 2 Screen printed strike poster from the 1969 student protests. Students printed the posters in the basement of Harvard's University Hall.   fig. 3 Strike poster from May 68, a period of civil unrest in France in response to capitalist social trends. Strikes and demonstrations began in May 1968 and continued for seven weeks.   fig. 4 Strike poster in the form of a language lesson from the 1969 student protests at Harvard.

3

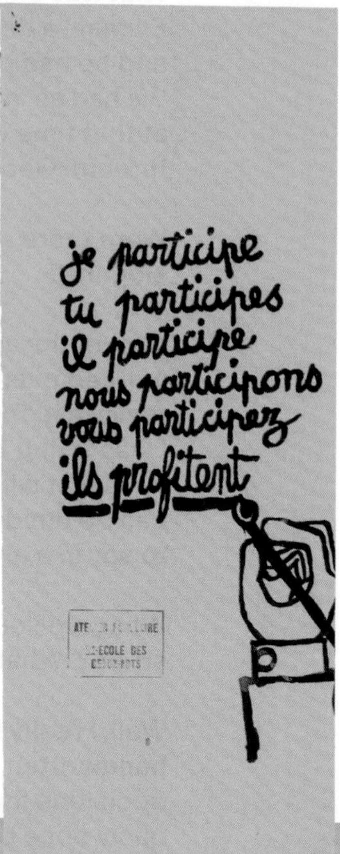

2

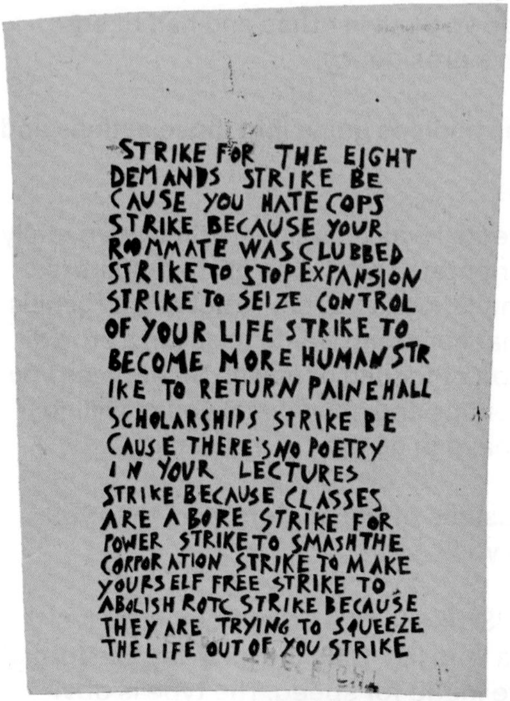

STRIKE FOR THE EIGHT
DEMANDS STRIKE BE
CAUSE YOU HATE COPS
STRIKE BECAUSE YOUR
ROOMMATE WAS CLUBBED
STRIKE TO STOP EXPANSION
STRIKE TO SEIZE CONTROL
OF YOUR LIFE STRIKE TO
BECOME MORE HUMAN STR
IKE TO RETURN PAINE HALL
SCHOLARSHIPS STRIKE BE
CAUSE THERE'S NO POETRY
IN YOUR LECTURES
STRIKE BECAUSE CLASSES
ARE A BORE STRIKE FOR
POWER STRIKE TO SMASH THE
CORPORATION STRIKE TO MAKE
YOURSELF FREE STRIKE TO
ABOLISH ROTC STRIKE BECAUSE
THEY ARE TRYING TO SQUEEZE
THE LIFE OUT OF YOU STRIKE

je participe
tu participes
il participe
nous participons
vous participez
ils profitent

4

Lesson 1: Conjugation
for Subjugation.

I restructure

you restructure

he
she } restructures
it

we restructure

you restructure

they control

Lesson 2: Conjugation
for Liberation.

I strike

you strike

he
she } strikes
it

we win

you win

they lose

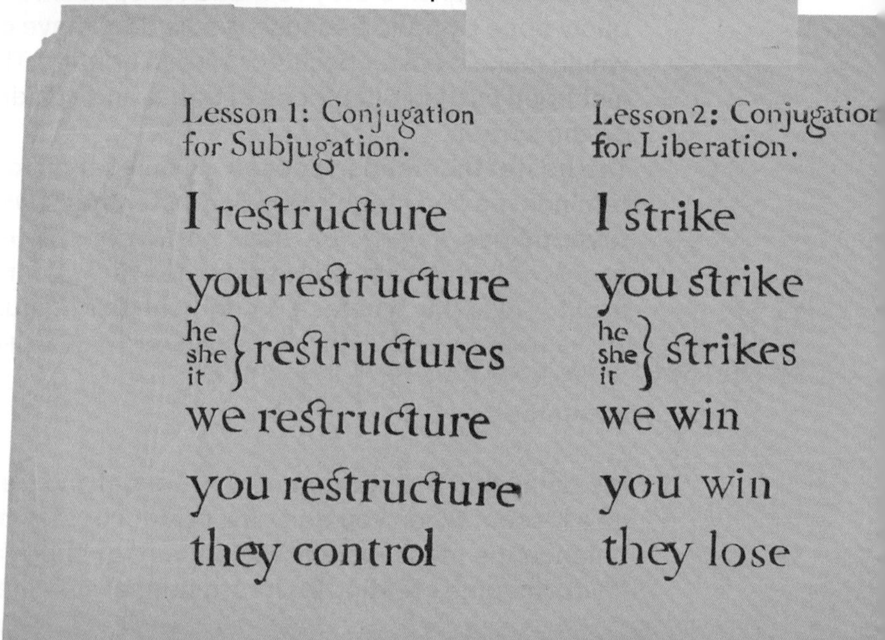

HARVARD UNIVERSITY STRIKE POSTERS

how much of it is going to be focused on image versus the fine print?

DA

It depends on the context. I imagine that the Harvard posters were proliferating within the place, maybe in public spaces, going up on message boards or around buildings on campus. Photos from the protest show 11,000 people gathered at the stadium, but they're not all standing there holding up signs. I think people in crowds holding signs for one another marks the current moment since Trump. For these Harvard posters, it feels like they're more about supporting and perpetuating the collective mood.

AW

The Harvard strike wasn't a typical labor strike because there weren't workers withholding labor to achieve a goal. It was students who were withholding attendance of class so that the university couldn't function.

DA

It was a general strike where everything and everyone stopped, rather than a union-sanctioned bureaucratic strike. The students exerted collective power by withholding whatever relationship they had to Harvard. There was no formal negotiation. Do you know how it was sustained and who was leading?

AW

One account I found said that undergraduates asked a cool-seeming PhD student to run the meeting at the stadium. The initial formal action was a product of the SDS, but after the University Hall occupation, the structure was very much of the moment. I think this was a real demonstration of student power. One of the remarkable things about the 1969 strike was that the students got their demands. Nowadays, I tend to fear that participating in student action could affect my professional outcomes. Collective action may upset professors who have the power to give out jobs. Students today face increasingly high expectations, like no resume gaps, which may be different from those of students in 1969. I'm curious, have you felt that fear? And if so, did you make a choice to overcome it?

DA

I made a decision to go into academia where I felt that taking action wouldn't be an issue. Times have changed, but whenever I would go for some corporate job, the fact that I was involved in leftist stuff would actually be a plus. That's also a testament to the ineffectiveness of the left at the time. People didn't really see it as a threat. You could say, "I'm an anarchist!" and, "Burn shit down," or whatever, but it never really felt like it was going to happen. In the last ten years, the left has been gaining traction, and now people don't discount it as easily. There is less patience for actual provocation. Culture workers, such as museum workers, are organizing now. Adjunct professors are organizing.

AW

This shift of new professions unionizing seems related to a rebranding of unions as a necessity in professions that require advanced degrees.

DA

That is a shift. I was active in the Democratic Socialists of America (DSA) after Trump was elected. A lot of people joining the DSA were office workers who were just beginning to see themselves as workers. I think that there has been a rebranding, or an acknowledgement that when you're working in a contemporary art museum and you're an art handler and you're making $30,000 a year, you're taught to think of that as a privileged job. But you're really not making enough to live on. When you don't have health insurance and you're just trying to act cool by not going to the doctor and not eating well, that's not sustainable. I feel like there is some type of rebranding that's happening writ large. It's happening with unions but also with socialism and the left.

AW

Do you think that this change is reflected in the aesthetic materials produced by unions? Have you seen a poster and thought, "Oh, this is a poster for millennials."

DA

Old-school leftists often don't want things to look too designed because it seems to play into consumer desires, and the left for so long has framed itself as being anti-consumer. Recently I think there's been more of an embrace of the tools of consumerism as a means to sell this political, ideological position. People are saying, "Social media is here. How can we make use of it to transmit information?" A group called Detroit Will Breathe used Instagram really well during protests following the death of George Floyd. They immediately had tens of thousands of followers. Their posts were black frames with white text in sans serif, saying things like, "There will be a mass meeting today, Wednesday, six o'clock." They would post it at noon, and two thousand people would show up.

AW

Do you think the effect would've been ruined if they used a serif?

DA

Whoever was making those was just making them.

HARVARD UNIVERSITY STRIKE POSTERS

You have professional-level graphic design skills. The students in 1969 had a general knowledge of design, but for them it was about bringing some skill to an instinctual, expedient scenario that produced the protest imagery.

DA

I mean, I have the fonts. I have the software. It looks like the students were doing stuff by hand, which is also interesting. The Harvard posters look like they're made by people with artistic sensibilities.

AW

It seems like the designers just said, "Okay. Strike." The design process involved writing the slogan. Have you had experiences like that?

DA

Mostly I end up writing the slogan. If you're making a poster, you don't have much real estate. Whatever image you produce, it ends up standing in for the issue itself. It does feel like a lot of pressure.

AW

Many designers have this hope that they're going to find some way to pay for their life, and then they're going to do more pro-gressive work or leftist work on the side. We don't have a lot of knowledge of how to make the progressive work a full-time gig. Designers are often pushed to draw a line between financial comfort and intellectual alignment with their work. How do you balance professional ambition with personal beliefs?

DA

I'm sure that if you're coming out of architecture school, you can be faced with paths where you think, "I can't in all good faith do this. I don't want to be building in this place or using the labor that is required for this project." Then you go in another direc-tion. It's a series of those decisions. Before I went to graduate school, I worked at an ad agency in New York, doing work for Frito-Lay and Pantene and Covergirl, or whatever. After school, I couldn't see myself working at an agency. There was a poli-tical element to it; I just didn't want to be a part of that. I ended up in academia. I have a lot of conversations with friends, who are also in academia and on the left, who just feel a bit complicit because we think academia is less bad than other industries, but we're also in academia on the backs of students with huge amounts of debt.

AW

In architecture particularly, there's a specific model of practice that's built around being an academic, having students who work for you, who are subsidized by the university. I think it's seen as the way to pursue your own creative work. But that work itself is still somehow related to the market of architecture and the market of academia. You're still trying to figure out a way to sell your work to someone.

DA

You have to figure out how to chart your path. What we often want is to have agency over what we're doing. The worst is when you're working someplace and you're doing something that you really object to.

AW

Where do you think the image and communication side of protests and organizing is going in the future?

DA

Identity design is important. Not in a corporate branding way. But figuring out how to represent the masses to themselves is what the most effective political graphics always do. Even during the Russian Revolution, Lenin talked about his political role as the mouthpiece of the people. That's what Emory Douglas was able to do with the Black Panthers.[4] He was a Panther, so he

Emory Douglas was the minister of culture for the Black Panthers and the art director for their newsletter. Douglas created many of the group's iconic images.

just understood what the Panthers were about, and he could represent the Panthers to themselves. That's what the role of the graphic should always be. At Wayne State, I want to rebrand our union. I'm nervous about it because I've only been there for a couple of years, but we need a new website. I had been in our union for some years but didn't even know the name of it when I offered to redesign our logo. I was like, "This can't be right. AAUP-AFT Local 6075?"

AW

A rebrand is a revitalization and expansion of a union. Consolidating some of that information makes a lot of sense, I think.

DA

It's about how you create a collective mood. Let's say we represent 1,700 people. How do you make people feel like this is you, you're in this thing? That's where identity design can really help. It helps you feel like you belong.

AW

One thing I struggle to imagine, as a designer in these new unions, is what an architect's strike would look like. If we said, "We're not going to do architecture," would anyone care? It's a little scary.

fig. 6 Poster handmade by students for the 1969 Harvard strike.   *fig.* 7 Poster from the 1969 Harvard strike.

6

HARVARD UNIVERSITY STRIKE POSTERS

I know. It feels the same way with graphic design. With architects unionizing and recognizing themselves as workers, it's also about aligning yourself with the broader union movement. At Wayne State, where I work, I feel like one of the most important areas of labor organizing is our coalition of unions on campus. We have monthly meetings with the building engineers, custodial union, and the graduate student union. That connection feels key. Also, architects do have power. This is a crass way to put it, but I think as higher-income laborers, you can wield influence within the larger affiliate. For example, we have doctors in our union who make a lot of money, so they pay a lot of dues. The state affiliates pay attention to our union because even if we don't have so many people, we pay a lot in dues.

A fiscal influence, it's a real thing. In architecture we have a new union, the first architecture group in 80 years to unionize.

Yeah, I've heard about that.

Workers at SHoP Architects in New York tried to unionize, but they failed because they received a lot of pushback from management. Then one of their employees went to Bernheimer Architecture, which only has 22 people, where a new union was created and voluntarily recognized. Have you been in a union that was in a similar setting?

Actually, I have this crazy experience being management in a small union, because my union, AAUP-AFT Local 6075, has staff that we pay through our dues, and they unionized. My predecessor gave them voluntary recognition but didn't negotiate a contract. When we negotiated, it ended up being pretty bureaucratic, and we haggled a lot over things that felt hypothetical. Unfortunately, I feel like it gave me insight into what it's like to be a manager, which I didn't really want. I just want to be a burn-it-all-down person. That said, voluntary recognition and being able to negotiate a contract collectively makes your job better, even at a small scale.

As president of the AAUP-AFT Local 6075 at Wayne State, you're dealing simultaneously with Detroit, a historical union town that has many years of established organizing practices, a brand new union that's very small and is still establishing its practices, a legacy union that has been around for decades, and renewed interest in union organizing from younger workers questioning established practices. A lot of culture workers and academics have never considered that they would be union workers. What do you think people who are engaging with unions for the first time have to learn from the history of unions?

DA

I've been confronted with the history of established unions. It's very legalistic and feels pretty far from that 1969 strike moment. I hope that the new wave of unionized workers brings fresh energy and bigger demands. Long-established unions don't strike. You're discouraged from rocking the boat. Unions involve politics, but I think the new wave of people unionizing should take their power. Recognize that if you come into the union, whichever group you're affiliated with, go in and try to shift things. Focus on your members. If your members are complaining about something, take it seriously and push that.

AW

The spirit of 1969 feels like it could be coming back. Do effective strikes happen outside of union contexts now?

DA

I think these rolling strikes happening everywhere in higher education are pointing in that direction. It feels like we're moving toward a crisis point. At what point are we at the crisis? Are we there now? It's felt this way since I was in graduate school, and even before that. We are taking on so much debt, and it feels like there's a drumbeat. The UC system had 48,000 people out on strike. The New School had the longest strike they've ever had. Columbia had the big strike. Eastern Michigan University was out. When you look historically at how things develop, it feels like something is building. We're headed somewhere.

Theaster Gates & Karel Miler's 'Actions'

Isabel Lewis & Theaster Gates

Let's begin.

ISABEL LEWIS

The first time I saw your work, I was nineteen and living in Portland, Oregon. I was taking a sculpture class, and the professor showed us a documentary about your practice. At the time, I was thinking about the way space is affected, how there's always a social aspect to spatial construction. Your work helped me open the door to the field I'm in now, design and landscape architecture.

Recently, this came full circle, because I went to see *Showing Up*, a film about a young woman, a sculptor, who works at an art school in Portland, which I think is based on the Oregon College of Art and Craft.[1] It brought me back to this very specific time

Showing Up, directed by Kelly Reichardt, with performances by Michelle Williams, Hong Chau, and Andre Benjamin (A24, 2023).

and place, this memory of living in that city and trying to figure out what sculpture meant to me. So it had a great impact on me when I saw in the end credits that you contributed art to the film. I was thinking we could start by talking about how memory informs your work.

TG

This happens for me too. Art and artists, they follow us through our lives. The more we learn about ourselves and the more experiences we have, sometimes a work of art shows up and carries a different meaning. It might mean more, it might mean less, but it continues to haunt us and be a part of us. For me, buildings, spaces, and materials also have that haunting effect. No matter what an object is, even the paint that you buy at a store, everything has history. It has an origin story. It has an eternity that precedes you. When you think about acrylic paint or oil paint, even if it's new, it has a history: the tube that it's in wasn't made today. Those processes are in fact part of a found or reclaimed identity, even though it's a new paint. You buy new wood at Home Depot, and it is not new wood. It's sometimes preexisting wood that's been planed again, it's a tree that has a history, an origin story. For me, saying that a thing is new or has history, it's everything. You can connect the fact that everything has a history and a narrative to, let's say, a Buddhist or an Africanist religious belief around animism, or the idea that things have life inside of them. I think what I'm interested in is participating in the truth of the life that is within things. The more I spend time with materials, the more I think, "Oh, yes, my dad was a roofer. Yes, roofing paper and the materials of roofing are important to me because of that history." But I also think that those materials have a life of their own, and that if I spend time deeply thinking about that life, then great things could happen with those materials. The South Side of Chicago wasn't born impoverished. The buildings that are currently abandoned, they weren't always abandoned. Those buildings have life in them, and it feels like my job is to recognize, exhume, and celebrate the great lives of these spaces. The more I believe the life these buildings have lived was important, the more I want to preserve this, the more I feel like, "This thing deserves to live, deserves to continue to live."

IL

I love that idea of reembodying a place or an image. The striking thing about this set of photos is how physical they feel. I have this bodily response where I imagine myself in these positions and how these things feel. There's a natural tendency to want to bring life into inanimate objects.

TG

Absolutely.

IL

It also reminds me of paint, oil paint in particular. We have these names like Siena or Umbrian Brown, and those come from the land. That's the color of dirt in Siena. These materials are defined by their most fundamental origins.

TG

Yeah. For every color that's a natural color, there's a plant or a mineral or an insect or a bark or a root that's being crushed and ground to produce the thing that then allows us to produce beauty. I think that those processes and those roots, they have their own beauty. Let's pull up an image, Isabel.

IL

I'm drawn to *Limits*, as with many of these images, because there's so much movement that's implied but not ever shown. You see the beginning and the end of an action, but everything in between is just inferred. I think it goes back to what we were saying about time and timelessness, too. We think of performance as a time-based art, but in its documentation, it becomes a moment completely out of time. When I look at this, I feel it in my body, and it becomes much more spatial than anything else, much more corporal.

TG

I also think that we're not necessarily analyzing the photograph itself, but the choices behind it. In 1973, Ektachrome was already available.[2] We were already in good and saturated color, but to

Ektachrome was a high-quality color film first produced by Kodak in the 1940s.

have this image in black and white adds to the austerity, meditation,

KAREL MILER'S "ACTIONS"

fig. 1 *Limits*, 1973   fig. 2 *Either — or*, 1972

1

2

simplicity, it makes those contrasts pop even more.

The artist, Karel Miler, was a Zen Buddhist. That stayed with him throughout his life, even after he stopped working as an artist. A lot of these images are meant to be a translation of poetry or meditation into a representative image. I wonder what you would end up with if you were to translate these images back into language.

Measurement is language in that you're taking a somewhat arbitrary sense of space, and you're codifying space with lines, and then you're giving those lines a shared understanding, so that we all agree to what a foot is or what a meter is, what a yard is, we agree to what a millimeter is, and as a result of our shared vocabulary, we're able to then translate information across time.

Does translation feel like an adequate way to describe how you move through different scales, from pottery to neighborhoods to larger urban structures?

I think about translation all the time, Isabel. I do. Sometimes when I'm making a work of art and I sit down with a journalist and they look at a tar painting, the first thing they say is, "So your dad was a roofer?" It's like, "Well, yes," but the thing that I'm trying to convey is not necessarily about my relationship with my father. There are other, more sophisticated codes embedded in these materials, not just one prescription.

Translation also has to do with our ability to deeply interpret the meaning of a word or moment. I think about translation in the sense that art is a stand-in for my words. It's a set of codes that goes without the need for my body, and it's able to say things, sometimes simple things, sometimes more complicated things. That's cool.

I recently wrote an essay about a dear friend of mine named Tony Lewis, an artist who uses language in his drawings, and it led me to look up the history of shorthand.[3] It seems like an ab-

Tony Lewis is a Chicago-based artist whose practice concerns semiotics, abstraction, and site specificity. He has exhibited at the Museum of Contemporary Art, Cleveland; Museo Marino Marini, Florence, Italy; and the Hirshhorn Museum and Sculpture Garden, Washington, D.C.

straction, but people who understand it can translate shorthand into language. If people across languages learn the same shorthands, then you can sometimes know universal shorthand without having to know the language. All of these modes are modes of translation and interpretation. It requires that you have

KAREL MILER'S "ACTIONS"

a base knowledge of something, and then you add to that base knowledge a symbol that is universalized. In that sense, Tony's work reminds me of this international code. It reads as abstraction, but only because most people don't read shorthand. I'm saying so much right now, Isabel, I'm so sorry.

IL

No, no, it's really wonderful.

TG

If we go for a second to the image titled *Measuring*, what I love about it is he's not only trying to set up the limits of his body, like between his body and a crevice, or a crevice and the rise of a stair. I think these things are so relevant for landscape architecture in that sense, because the rise seems incredibly human. When you think about stately stairs, the rise is often short, sometimes the run is super deep. You actually have to take two or three steps for each tread, and it's interesting to think about how when it gets past the foot, when it gets to three feet or five feet, it reads as grand because it's bigger than our body.

IL

Form and the body have such an interesting relationship to scale. All those books of the architectural standards say that a countertop is going to be this high and a cabinet is going to be this high because a typical body looks like this, but then my mother can't reach any glasses from the top shelf because she's not a five-foot-nine male. It's worth subverting those expectations to measure space by atypical metrics. I made a Klein Diagram a little while ago about tables and chairs.[4] A baby sitting in a high-

The Klein Diagram is a four-group graph describing how elements are related to each other and their opposing forms. It was famously used by Rosalind Krauss in her seminal 1979 essay "Sculpture in the Expanded Field" to describe the relation of sculpture and architecture.

chair, that's a chair and a table in one element, with a very prescribed use. But if you're perched over the kitchen counter, eating takeout from a container, you're not in a chair nor at a table, and you're not using the counter as intended. It's that individual expression, I think, that really makes a place belong to someone.

TG

Well, last summer just before going to Japan, I went to a yoga class and the yoga instructor asked, "What do you want to get out of the class?" I said, "I need to be able to sit cross-legged for two to three hours." What I needed most from yoga was to help me respect the social customs of the dinner table. I knew that moving from my cultural predisposition to a Japanese cultural predisposition would require work, exercise, stretching. I think that sometimes architecture and landscape architecture

fig. 3 *Grating*, 1974

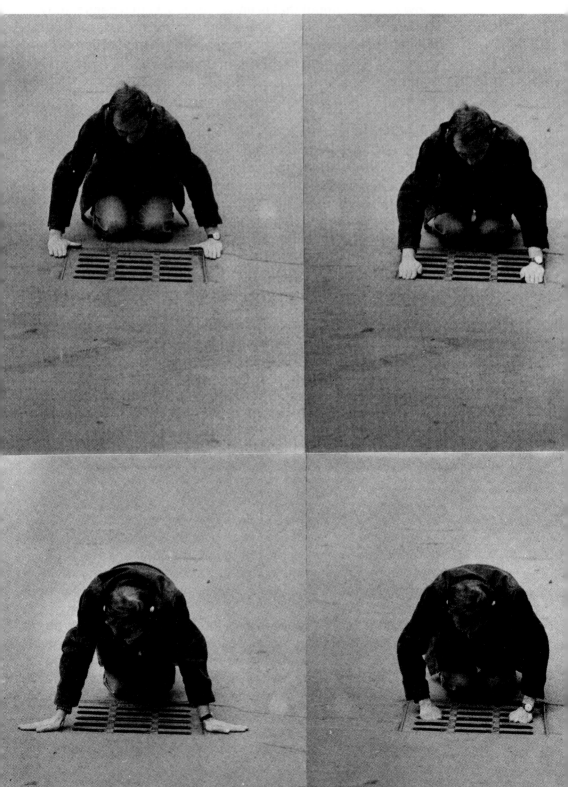

can inform our new cultural norms. It could allow us ways of getting out of ourselves and maybe new ways of thinking about what dinner could be.

IL

The reason why I ended up including this image, *Grating*, was because it made me reevaluate the simple idea of holding something in your hand, a perfect weight, a textural variation. By taking a record out of its sleeve or by thinking about how you're going to shape a pot or play an instrument or cook a meal, all of these things are fundamentally about how we touch the world. It's not something that's exportable or translatable.

TG

Touch is important because it is one of our first phenomena. Whether it's the first touch when a baby is born, or consistent touch as a baby ages, or the ability to process information like hot and cold, it's the way we learn to be in the world and encounter our limits. These images speak to my own interests in the ways they demonstrate how having a sense of how texture affects a viewer of art. People don't want to just see things; they also want to touch them and know them. To see is to know, but to touch is to also know.

IL

Yes, and with the Archive House and the Johnson Publishing Company artifacts, you could make the argument that these objects should be preserved in a museum. But there's something about flipping through an object that's very different.

TG

Yes, and back to this conversation about the different ways that architectural archetypes show up, who's to say that the Listening House isn't a more perfect museum?[5] Because we have the

The Listening House is one of several abandoned properties on the South Side of Chicago whose use Gates reimagined. Today, it houses a record collection of over 8000 LPs with cultural significance to the Black community in Chicago.

ability to touch things—turning the pages of a book, looking closely at a glass lantern slide—we can be more than just witnesses to them by being witnesses through them.

The truth is, when you advance in your research at universities like Yale and Harvard and the University of Chicago, you can gain access to special collections and touch things that other people can't. I think that sometimes touch is also about who has access and who doesn't.

IL

Even with this magazine, it's partly because we're all at the Harvard Graduate School of Design that we are able to have access to

41

these people and to these objects. It's a privilege. I think the hope is that by doing and sharing this work, we're making the process at least somewhat more accessible. But it is true that touch is something that you're very lucky to access. I think there's probably a lot of lack of touch in the world right now.

TG

For me at least, as I was building the Listening House, Archive House, and Black Cinema House, and ultimately the Stony Island Arts Bank, I was definitely thinking about a person's experience of these different spaces. [6] The experience of that has everything

The Stony Island Bank was vacant from the 1980s until 2015, when it was reopened by the Rebuild Foundation, a nonprofit founded and led by Gates to rehabilitate abandoned spaces on the South Side of Chicago. Today, the Bank serves as a local hub for artistic innovation and archival research, housing collections of music, film, magazines, and other significant cultural artifacts.

to do with trying to create more access to the place, more access to people. I feel like we've at least been successful in helping people gain access. I'm quite proud of that.

IL

I've been thinking a lot about the way that clay in particular holds memory. It holds fingerprints, and the act of throwing a pot is so intensely physical, really, really hard work. When you hold something in your hands like that and it's shaped by your hands, it has your imprint on it. But it's interesting to think about the way that that is scalable through other materials as well.

TG

Absolutely. It's reasonable that when we're doing renovation projects, if we take out a stone, like a terra-cotta cornerstone, from a building, we can see the marks of the maker. But they might also put in some funny anecdote, or write their name or the date, because these are not actually anonymous objects. They're anonymous to us because the histories of those materials haven't always been carried forward. But in fact, from a pot to a large structure, objects often carry the remnants of people's touch. If you look close enough at most buildings, you'll see the traces of the people who made them.

IL

This is relevant to something I was working on last semester about Julie Bargmann's work in rehabilitating toxic landscapes. In a landscape project, there's this dual action of not erasing history but honoring it while also acknowledging that land often has a complicated past. How do we preserve memory in built environments or urban landscapes in a way that feels authentic?

TG

I think sometimes art and conceptual practices can help us on that journey. Sometimes, and I think this is what we'll get to with

KAREL MILER'S "ACTIONS"

these photographs, performance and conceptual ideas help us tackle these bigger questions by putting the body present in ways that implicate a site, make you feel more compassion toward the site because of the complexities of the things that happened there.

I remember when Cabrini-Green in Chicago was being torn down.[7] There was concern that poor people were being dis-

Cabrini-Green was a public housing development built by the Chicago Housing Authority (CHA) following the Second World War. Due to neglect and a lack of financial support from the CHA, the development fell into disrepair and became a symbol of urban blight. Its demolition was completed in 2011.

placed, largely poor Black people, because that land had become some of the most important land in the city for its adjacency to downtown. It's like, "Well, Black people still deserve the right to live in a place that they've been living in for the last fifty years, sixty years, for which nobody gave a damn." The site has changed over time, but the people haven't. What do you do when time has shifted people's stigma of a place?

People who lived in Cabrini Green deserve the right to continue to live there, even if the land is now worth a lot of money. When they were excavating, there was a lot of clay underground. I remember just trying to get access to that site and that clay, to use it as a stand-in for the people who once lived there.

IL

I think there's this notion that a landscape intervention won't do harm. It's complicated because there's one lens that focuses more on the rights of the biome and another on the rights of people. Of course, they go hand in hand.

TG

We look to landscape architecture as the solution to neutralizing space and time. It starts with large projects that are government or municipality projects, but then you have private developers and privately-owned public spaces.[8] In these moments, we

Privately-owned public spaces (POPS) are plazas, atria, or similar areas, typically in urban centers, that are open to the public while being owned and maintained by private corporations, often as a way to circumvent zoning restrictions or floor-area ratio regulations.

need landscape to give us something that is not an office building, not a residential thing. But that safe passage route or that new bike lane or that grove of trees is sometimes still a disruptive act of transferring a community space from one of people in need to one of people that have a tremendous amount. I think protecting green and public spaces is important, and also not using green space or landscape as the thing that disintegrates a certain community continuity is important.

fig. 4 Identification, 1973

KAREL MILER'S "ACTIONS"

What I'm trying to get across is that people can think of landscape as very politically neutering. It's like, of course, who wouldn't want landscape beauty in their neighborhood? But I do think that there's a tendency when any project is approached with this developer-down, top-down approach that erases the individual user. Maybe the only way to really approach this idea is from the inside out, moving from what you can shape with your hands to eventually what can shape you.

TG

I think we're saying the same thing, Isabel, that every urban tool can be a divisive, derisive device that separates and disconnects as much as it can be a tool that aggregates and reconnects. There is no neutral tool, including landscape architecture, and I think it's really powerful that you're able to see that. There will be moments where you'll be on big projects, and it'll be like, "Fuck!" When we build these new cities, we haven't given any thought yet to where people are going to commune. They're building apartment buildings and they're building bus depots and transit things, but they haven't thought about places of worship. They haven't thought about the park where people might do yoga.

IL

Yeah, at least in the US, I feel like it can be a very capitalistic way of thinking. We consider how people can get to work but not about where they can get together. How do you think the work you've done in creating cultural archives supports community?

TG

Well, right now, I'm in the center of downtown Chicago. You get used to seeing the same shit in every city, you know what I mean? We could be in New York right now, we could be in LA, we could be in Paris, we could be in London. One thing that's interesting about the Arts Bank is that it shows up as an unexpected and autonomous form. Its use is so different from the typical use that's evident on our urban streets. What makes the city special to me is the fact that there are things autonomous to that city. It's not enough just to have the archive, it needs to populate the block in the same way that any other storefront could.

I think the Dorchester Projects gave me an opportunity to install my own interpretation of the architectural image of a block.[9]

The Dorchester Projects is a foundational expression of Gates's interdisciplinary practice, in which urban design, archival preservation, and neighborhood engagement come together. In 2009, Gates purchased and then rehabilitated a set of neglected houses on Chicago's South Side into vibrant cultural spaces, including the Archive House, the Listening House, and the Black Cinema House. In addition to serving the local community, these spaces are a model of positive urban restoration and collective action.

Inside that architectural image are a set of things that are totally specific to what I care about. I love looking at images. I love looking at images with others. I love making music with images behind me. I love learning about other people's histories through objects. In that sense, the bank became a place of congregation and shared values. Then it leads you to realize, "Oh, I don't even have to go to the bank to look at these kinds of images. My grandmama has images on her wall that I never pay attention to—who are those old people on my grandma's wall?" Before you know it, you start to have a new appreciation, not only for other people but for your own freaking family.

IL

I think one of the things that's particularly beautiful about photography is the dissonance between the original event and the reception of its documentation. Sometimes the documentation can spark a reimagining of its own in which you start building a narrative around the things that came together.

TG

Absolutely. Images test the limits of a person, but they're also about the deep recording of a specific moment. When you're making the image, you don't necessarily know that it is going to be important, but we're looking at curbs and streets that may not exist anymore, buildings for performances that don't exist anymore. But an artist punctuated this site, and we have proof of its existence. With the artist, we have a way to remember a thing that occurred.

IL

We take these things as ready-made. The photograph is there, the paint is there, the canvas is stretched, et cetera. But then, when you remove an action from its documentation, it's something completely independent. I'm thinking back to something you said in a TED Talk, that when you started the Archive House in the Dorchester Projects, even just sweeping it became a performance.

TG

There's a tension and a relationship between the gesture that one performs and the document that captures that gesture, and then eventually, what that documentation means for the future. I sometimes want to be able to go back and show people a moment when all I could afford was eggs and mushrooms and potatoes from the local market. It was food you had to eat that day, it was almost on its way out. As a result, the cost per pound was so cheap that I could buy five pounds of mushrooms for $2.50 and I could make a big frittata. I wish I had evidenced those

KAREL MILER'S "ACTIONS"

days more. I wish somebody had taken a picture of me making my frittata and slowly letting that pan get hot, because people assume I've always had a chef, or I've always had handlers or some shit. I'm like, "No, that's actually the last five years that I've had help." But those gestures, those moments really matter. Me, when I could drop it like it's hot, I could dance. It's difficult for my nephews to imagine me partying, because the gestures that I make today as an older adult, they're so different from the gestures that I made when I was 25. All I can say to them is, your uncle was the life of the party, trust me.

Shannon Mattern & Nancy Graves Maps

Areti Kotsoni & Shannon Mattern

ARETI KOTSONI

Shannon, how do you define a map?

SHANNON MATTERN

I wish I had prepared for that question! I've been teaching map-related classes for the past decade, and the challenge I always face is encouraging my students to break away from the traditional cartographic understanding of mapping. Can we consider data visualization, for example, to be a form of mapping, or does that stretch the definition too far? Must mapping involve a spatial dimension or a specific topographic representation? When we think about the relationships between things, are we drawing boundaries or contours within a field? What is the value of thinking expansively and inclusively about mapping as a concept?

AK

In your essay "How to Map Nothing," I was struck by the inclusion of various perspectives from female cartographers, such as Mei-Po Kwan, which shed light on different approaches to mapping.[1] It beautifully highlighted how mapping goes beyond the

Shannon Mattern, "How to Map Nothing," *Places Journal* (March 2021).

simple representation of existing realities; it has the power to generate entirely new worlds. It was a thought-provoking revelation that opened my eyes to the immense possibilities and creative potential that maps hold.

SM

I strongly believe that maps are intricately tied to spatial relationships, but their purpose extends beyond mere representation. They have the potential to enact or perform those relationships. There are countless verbs and gerunds that can fill in the blank. Maps can represent existing relations, bring them into existence through various representational modes, perform, enact, and even embody them. This broader definition of mapping allows for a more comprehensive understanding of the interconnectedness between points, lines, areas, or any spatial concept. The beauty lies in the flexibility and versatility of the verbs that can be applied to these relations.

AK

This brings us to Nancy Graves's maps of the earth, the moon, and Mars. I find her maps fascinating as they showcase spatial relationships of various kinds, and they pique my interest in your perspective on topological maps versus topographic maps. In my work, I've been grappling with what type of maps would be most effective in illustrating the division of Cyprus. Nicosia is a compact city with remarkable Venetian walls that encircle it. Despite the city's expansion beyond these walls, they remain

fig. 1 *Riphaeus Mountains Region of the Moon, 1972*

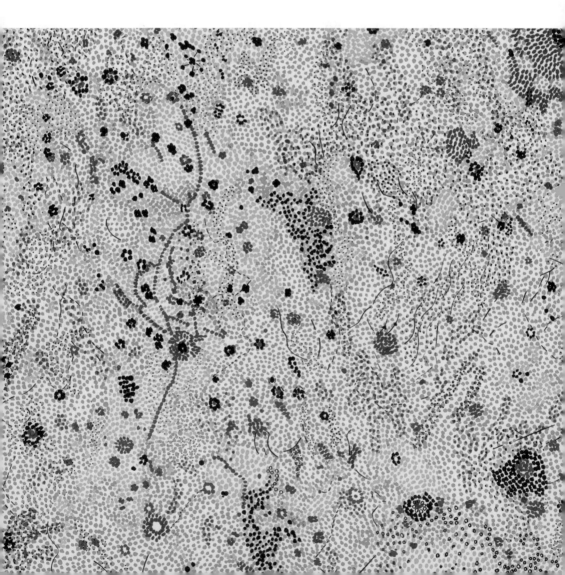

intact, forming a perfect circle that splits the city in the middle. Within the buffer zone, which traverses the city's historic area enclosed by the walls, the distance is roughly two meters. This allows for visual contact from one side of the city to the other. The streets are not obstructed by walls or physical barriers but rather by sandbags, wires, and barrels—an improvised method of blocking access and creating a symbolic border.

My aim was to understand how individuals, particularly those of marginalized genders, perceive urban space within this context of barriers. It's fascinating to consider that despite the proximity, it was not until 2003 that people could interact and communicate freely. For three decades, even though they were just two meters apart, their interactions were restricted due to the closed blocks and crossings. I wanted to explore how the perception of these barriers have evolved since the opening of the crossings. Because of sovereign complexities, there seems to be limited movement, particularly from the south to the north. This creates a profoundly challenging and intricate narrative—a story that is incredibly difficult to navigate and understand.

SM

But it also highlights the tendency of most mapping endeavors to prioritize visualization, movement, and the assertion of territorial claims. When we consider a border like the one you described—impermeable in some aspects yet permeable in others—it calls for different mapping strategies and cartographic techniques. In this context, physical mobility from one side of the city to the other may not be feasible, requiring alternative approaches that account for these limitations and complexities. This prompts us to explore cartographic methods that go beyond traditional notions of mapping, as the focus shifts from bodily movement to the intricate dynamics of space and perception. But your sense of longing, your feeling of loss, transcends that border.

AK

Sound also has the ability to traverse borders, defying physical boundaries.

SM

Sound can travel across the barrier, and you can visually perceive what lies beyond it. So, how do you discover methods of capturing, not just visually but mentally, the fact that only certain categories of experience are blocked by the barrier, and others extend beyond it? All these different sensory elements have the potential to warp or transform our perception of topographic distance.

Another aspect to consider is technology's role in capturing sound, as seen in sound maps. Sound has the ability to convey certain truths, ways of being, and distinct characteristics of space that cannot be fully captured through purely factual cartographic representations. Exploring the use of sound recordings or digital sound maps, whether in a digital or performative context, presents an intriguing opportunity to capture space's spectral and imaginary elements.

Some individuals have developed remarkable walking tours that go beyond traditional maps. These tours involve performing the map through reenactments, on-site installations, or using locative media in various forms. By triggering specific audio files at particular locations, these technologies offer a means to capture multiple layers of placeness.

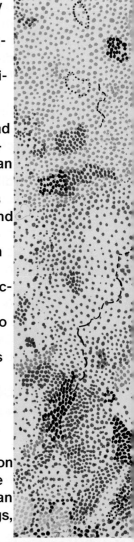

AK

Nancy Graves was a multitalented artist who, at 29 years old, was one of the first five female artists to exhibit at the Whitney Museum. What particularly intrigues me are the maps she crafted of the moon, the earth, and Mars. How should one consider researching and producing these maps? Should one take an improvisational and abstract approach based on their intuition as a researcher navigating the city?

SM

It depends on how you define research, because you could read all kinds of theory, you could read all kinds of cartographic history. I personally find exploring the works of map artists to be an equally important aspect of research. It allows me to examine different modes of aestheticization and experimental methods employed by artists. For instance, artists like Nancy Graves and Kate McLean, known for their sensory mapping, offer unique perspectives. There are artists who use embroidery or fabric in their mapping.

These are not just purely cosmetic choices. They all have affective dimensions that determine the topological nature of experiencing space. I find the most generative form of research is to see the different aesthetic techniques that map artists and cartographers use, which can capture more affective dimensions of space. Sure, you could read about it and read some theory about it, which might be illuminating in its own way, but I find that looking at as much art as possible is just as valuable a form of research.

AK

One of the highlights of Graves's exhibition is the renowned moon drawing, which was intended to be a vivid and expansive-scale representation. Its vibrant colors truly bring it to life. Artists can convey unique perspectives and emotions through their mappings,

NANCY GRAVES MAPS

fig. 2 Part of Sabine D. Region, Southwest Mare Tranquilitatis, 1972
fig. 3 Fra Mauro Region of the Moon, 1972

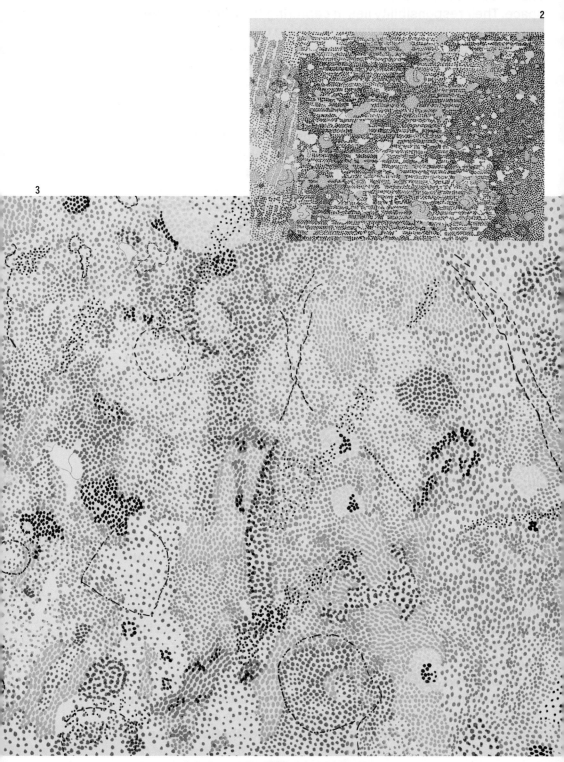

using aesthetics as a powerful tool to evoke certain feelings, challenge established norms, or explore alternative narratives of space. Their responsibility lies in capturing the affective dimensions of their subject matter and provoking thoughtful engagement and reflection. Is the artist responsible for producing visually appealing maps, while the scientist focuses on truth and objectivity? What is the responsibility of artists and scientists in their respective mappings and maps?

SM

They probably have different responsibilities given that their purpose for mapping and their audiences might be different. A scientist, for instance, might be producing maps to speak to other scientists, which requires adhering to certain conventions that facilitate accessibility and operationalization in specific contexts. Ideally, there should be a cross-pollination of ideas between artists and scientists. Artists excel at challenging the conventional norms of mapping rather than reinforcing them or reifying cartographic conventions. They prompt us to question the origins of data and the reasons behind the chosen modes of representation. Scientists also make aesthetic choices. Bobby Pietrusko and Laura Kurgan explore various aspects of maps, such as color selection, color schemes, graphic techniques for filling in certain areas, and even the choice of base maps.[2]

Bobby Pietrusko is an associate professor at the Weitzman School of Design at the University of Pennsylvania. He is an architect and composer based in Brooklyn, New York, and specializes in research on the historical and speculative design possibilities of environmental media. Laura Kurgan is a professor of architecture at the Graduate School of Architecture, Planning and Preservation (GSAPP) at Columbia University. She is also the director of Columbia's Master of Science in Computational Design Practices (MSCDP) program and the Center for Spatial Research, and she coordinates the curriculum of the GSAPP Visual Studies sequence.

AK

The selection of icons also holds significance as it can promote inclusivity or exclusivity.

SM

Absolutely! Indigenous mapping, for example, highlights the importance of place names and the use of specific typefaces that capture the essence of a location. The choice of particular typefaces can capture the character of place as well. These, again, are not purely aesthetic choices. They also have implications for the ontology, the beingness, and the epistemology of space. I'm engaging in speculative thinking here, but I believe that artists have a unique role—not necessarily a job but an obligation and an opportunity—to challenge and inspire us to question the apparent codification, rules, and conventions of cartography. Moreover, I think scientific mappers can gain valuable insights from artistic mappers, such as discovering that aesthetic choices can be made in ways that are more inclusive and recognizing that space is not solely defined by topography but also by its topological aspects. There is significant potential for cross-pollination between these different populations.

AK

My interest in political maps started during my architectural studies, when I delved into understanding the intricacies between the elements of a city and its infrastructure. Graves's drawing of the moon intrigued me greatly, particularly because of the fascinating interplay between the real and the imaginary, as well as the relationship between her artistic practice and the abstraction of scientific data. Interestingly, NASA was simultaneously unveiling photographs, maps, and drawings while Graves created her maps. This synchronicity added another layer of interest to the whole endeavor.

SM

Yes, there are myriad techniques people have applied to try to think about representing what may not be physically present, such as the historical, the erased, the imaginary, and the spectral. Deep mapping is one approach that draws inspiration from Indigenous traditions. There's "thick mapping," which Todd Presner talks about.[3]

Todd Presner is the chair of the Department of European Languages and Transcultural Studies at the University of California, Los Angeles and serves as special advisor to Vice Chancellor Roger Wakimoto in the Office of Research and Creative Activities.

AK

How can we establish connections between significant experiences, encompassing the lived realities of the urban population, and leverage technology to enhance their overall experiences?

SM

You can have a very data-driven base map onto which you layer the more subjective experiences, or you can use interactive mapping where you can turn on and off layers that will get at the palimpsestic nature of space. That is what my old urban media archaeology class was about. We were researching historical and contemporary media infrastructures in cities while simultaneously working with programmers and designers at Parsons to build an open-source mapping tool. This tool would allow us to map humanistic aspects, aiming to capture things like ambiguities, uncertainties, and erasures. A data-driven tech tool isn't really good at doing that, since it prefers hard and fast numbers and plotting points in specific geographic areas. We wanted to explore how to make the tool do things it wasn't originally meant to do, enabling us to capture these affective dimensions. That's where technology can be useful.

fig. 4 *Julius Caesar Quadrangle of the Moon, 1972*   fig. 5 *Montes Apenninus Region of the Moon, 1972*

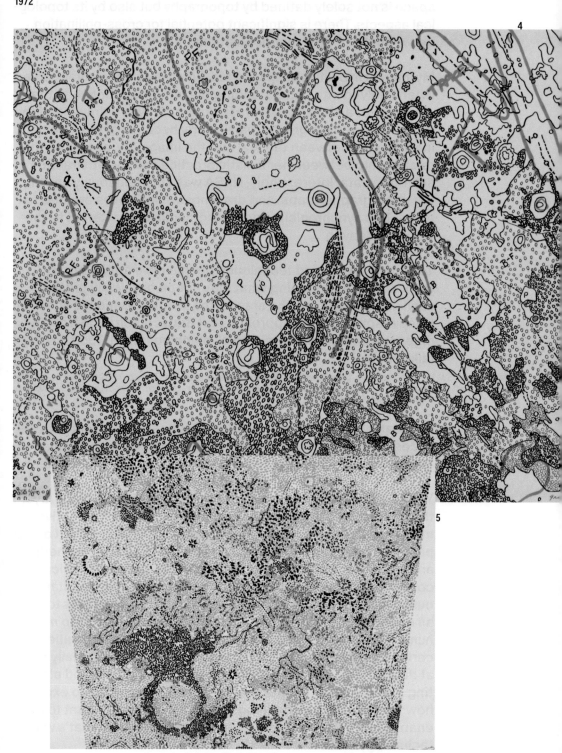

NANCY GRAVES MAPS

We map everything continuously.

A thing that I have learned through years of working with students on maps is that they often want to try to find one map that can capture the multiple layers of being in a space. And sure, the too-muchness, the overwhelming nature and volume of data can be part of an argument about intentional illegibility. It demonstrates the over-determined nature of place. That's one strategy: you can intentionally choose to load up a map with multimodal data points.

But you don't always have to do everything on one specific map. This is where I feel like atlases are useful, not only as a biblio-graphic form but as a metaphor to think about having multiple maps in a sequence that build on top of each other. Each map in an atlas could be in a different modality. One could be sound, one could be based on a performativity, another could be a more traditional cartographic map.

A video instead of photographs.

A book called *Sidewalk City* by Annette Miae Kim explores the sidewalk culture in Ho Chi Minh City and Hanoi.[4] The book show-

Annette M. Kim is an associate professor at the University of Southern California Sol Price School of Public Policy. She is also the director of the newly formed Spatial Analysis Lab (SLAB) at Price, which advances the visualization of the social sciences for public service through teaching, research, and public engagement.

cases the potential of using video essays and various experi-mental forms of cartography, each offering a unique narrative or argument about space. Since she focuses on informal uses of space, of course you're not going to rely on state-sanctioned, tech-nologically driven modes of mapping. She employs ephemeral and embodied forms of mapping to capture the essence of these improvisational, seasonal, and ephemeral spatial practices. In the book, there are compelling examples of how a photo essay, particularly when graphically designed and presented, can pos-sess a spatial quality. I have attended installations where photo essays were situated in physical spaces, guiding the viewer through a narrative by strategically placing the photos. These in-stallations create a microcosmic experience that captures a larger cartographic terrain. Thus, I believe that photo essays have the potential to serve as maps in their own right.

I am reminded of your paper "Learning from Lines," in which you explore the significance of data visualizations during the COVID-19 quarantine period.[5] I recall your statement that "photographs

Emily Bowe, Erin Simmons, and Shannon Mattern, "Learning from lines: Critical COVID data visualizations and the quarantine quotidian," *Big Data & Society* (July 2020).

serve as passive data visualization, illuminating the distinctive patterns of the virus." This made me wonder if you hold a similar perspective on the capabilities of photographs. I had previously believed that photographs could not be incorporated into actual technical mapping as a method or artifact, but this paper has prompted me to reassess my understanding of mapping and contemplate how I can create meaningful maps. Especially when researching spaces frequented by minority groups, various genders, and the queer community, there is a dilemma of how much one can reveal in terms of location. One needs to protect the privacy and safety of these spaces. Consequently, I find myself pondering how one can address conditions on the ground in these spaces and discuss these places without inadvertently exposing them.

SM

This strategy aligns with my research on mapping techniques over the years, particularly when it comes to activist mapping aimed at highlighting marginalized or vulnerable populations, whether human or nonhuman. In such cases, researchers often employ a variety of strategies. One approach involves intentionally introducing ambiguity or blurring the data. This can be achieved by using hazy representations, in which data points lack clear outlines. Another approach involves not using a base map at all, removing the topographic dimension, and focusing solely on showing topologies.

For example, in one of my mapping classes two springs ago, a student of mine was studying women's informal economies on the streets of Mumbai. She was cautious about disclosing the specific locations of their illicit businesses. Instead, she developed an interactive project that employed infinite horizontal scrolling. You encounter these people as she did while walking around her own self-defined route in the city. The project possessed spatiality, with a linear direction and implied geography, yet she deliberately refrained from providing exact locations or plotting them on a map. Hence, various approaches exist, from employing different modes of graphic representation for points, lines, and areas to eliminating or blurring the base map and even focusing on a loose set of spatial relations.

AK

It sounds like a scientific map and an artistic map at the same time.

NANCY GRAVES MAPS

Yeah. Another thing she wanted to do was use photographs as part of her fieldwork, but she did not want to show them because they revealed too much high-fidelity information, which could generate vulnerability. She had to translate all of her photographs into intentional illustrations that refused to show faces and certain identifying characteristics about people. Not only did she have this linear technique that removed the topography but she translated her photographs into another modality that refused high-fidelity representation.

AK

Perhaps this can be another definition of what a map is: a map is what you define it to be.

SM

I prefer that. But then you encounter individuals like Denis Wood, who, at first glance, might fit the stereotype of a white male cartographer rooted in a traditional understanding of maps.[6] Accord-

Denis Wood is an artist, author, cartographer, and a former professor of design at North Carolina State University.

ing to this perspective, maps are primarily associated with the state or governed by specific conventions that must be followed. Departing from these conventions might lead to an excessively flexible and ultimately meaningless definition of mapping. I prefer to think more capaciously about it.

AK

It's time to redefine the map's purpose, transforming it into a powerful tool for research and self-expression.

SM

Absolutely. I used to take my class on field trips to mapping platforms like Mapbox or CARTO, which are relatively user-friendly. During those visits, we extensively discussed the opportunities and risks associated with the democratization of cartography and the importance of expanding the boundaries of what a map can represent. However, one of the risks that emerged was the potential for individuals who are not well-versed in working with data, particularly those lacking statistical literacy, to encounter challenges. Understanding the established conventions can be beneficial as it allows us to intentionally push against them when necessary. While flexibility is valuable, it is essential to remain ethically mindful and intentional in our choices to prevent the introduction of inaccuracies or risks into the mapping process.

AK

A question at hand in relation to Graves's maps is whether we can educate individuals to think in a manner informed by feminism, encouraging them to critically examine the data they utilize and reveal their own positionalities.

SM

I would love to see that. The issue is that, in a certain context, people don't really have the time or the interest in that. If, for example, you're looking at a data visualization in the *New York Times*, you're not going to have a whole side article about how the data was harvested. Maybe on interactive versions on the website, there could be a little thing you click through to understand a colophon or the biography of the map itself. I consistently encourage my students to do this after they have completed constructing their atlases in my classes. Whether through an introduction, a postscript, or another suitable section, I urge them to integrate self-reflexivity into their work. Even if it isn't explicitly embedded within each map, they can still explore creative ways to incorporate this mode of self-critique within the atlas. Some students exhibit remarkable creativity and find methods to encourage the audience or viewer to engage in this practice of self-reflection alongside them, directly on the pages as they examine the maps together.

AK

I am intrigued by the integration of mapping and the mapping methods we have discussed into the field of design, particularly architecture. When beginning a project, we analyze the site through physical visits or other means, capturing photographs, taking measurements, and conducting various assessments. In essence, this process is akin to fieldwork. In the past, I often discarded these maps, designs, and sketches, deeming them useless. I have come to realize that the existing data and observations of the space at the site visit form the foundations of my design interventions. I am curious about how architectural pedagogy can become more inclusive, incorporating methodologies from other disciplines, particularly social sciences.

SM

As a non-designer, when I go to architecture creation centers, I am blown away by the visual facility of many students, especially in the data visualizations that precede a design proposal. Sometimes they're inscrutable to me. I know that they're beautifully rendered, but they don't convey a clear argument. Some people are fortunate to have professors who think critically about the available software, while others focus on using software as an out-of-the-box solution without much of a critical dimension. There's a lot of variability between classes and programs. I would love to see a lot more reflexivity, including people asking questions about the software they're using, the cartographic techniques they're employing, and the role of data visualization.

How can architects learn more from the social sciences? Well, I hope they're learning from mapping artists. There's sociology, and not all sociology is data-driven. Having greater data literacy can help them understand the sociology behind the dataset they're mapping, and this can inform the design they're proposing.

AK

Sometimes you find yourself in a situation where you, as a non-anthropologist, are teaching an anthropology class. This raises questions about how others perceive your work as anthropological.

SM

One thing that I found interesting when comparing design peda-gogy and anthropology pedagogy is the difference in the meaning of fieldwork. It seems that fieldwork is often fetishized in anthro-pology. That said, there's a lot of critical thinking about the ethics of fieldwork, about what it means to spend time in a place, about how you enter and then exit the field, and what your obligations are to the people and the ecologies you're working with. In a lot of design pedagogy, fieldwork means taking a day or two, or even just an afternoon, to gather information about the site.

I believe that adopting the anthropologists' perspective on fieldwork could be beneficial, even if designers cannot replicate the yearslong immersive experiences that anthropologists have. It would involve considering what insights they might be miss-ing out on due to the limitations they face. Additionally, partner-ing with social scientists could provide a more robust under-standing of the sites they're working with, offering valuable insights and perspectives.

AK

So perhaps an initial step for architects and designers is to ac-knowledge and understand the importance of cultivating empathy and inclusivity when it comes to gathering information about how people live and the specific environment in which they plan to intervene. It's crucial for them to recognize the need for such insights. We can explore ways to collaborate with others who can provide this essential information.

SM

Absolutely, yes. I think there's something about the depth and robustness of observation, not only with anthropologists, who can help you understand the human elements, but also ecologists. By spending time with landscape ecologists, designers can gain valuable insights about a space. Just imagine the wealth of knowledge they could generate by immersing themselves in a location for a month or even multiple years.

AK

It's an incredibly liberating experience for me because I face ethical dilemmas when presented with opportunities to work in unfamiliar locations, communities, cultures, and even languages. These limitations raise questions like, "Why was I chosen for this role?" and "How could I truly be of assistance in this position?" Of course, one can collaborate with others to conduct the work. By assembling a diverse team of experts from various fields, we can foster a project that can genuinely make a positive impact. This approach allows for the inclusion of individuals who possess the necessary language skills, cultural understanding, and expertise needed to create a comprehensive and effective solution for the community.

SM

Right. It's important to realize that you don't have to possess expertise in all areas within one mind. I know that many students doing fieldwork have a lot of qualms about the potential impact of their work. They are very concerned about not doing extractive research.

AK

This idea recalls the concept of feminist mapping that you discussed in "How to Map Nothing." The essence of feminist mapping lies in collaborating with the individuals directly involved in the mapping process, practicing care, and ensuring inclusivity. In essence, it involves acknowledging the agency of all those engaged in the process so that each person and artifact has a voice in shaping the work being conducted.

SM

Establishing a collaboration is not a skill that everybody has. I feel like this is another area where we need help and expertise. There's a way to do community engagement that's very formulaic, that involves just checking a box that says, "Yes, we fulfilled the obligation of engaging with the community." But I think that there are also some organizations, like Creative Reaction Lab in St. Louis, that really think from the perspective of communities that have historically been extracted from in order to think about how we can learn from the sensibilities of those communities and follow their leadership to build respectful collaborations.[7]

Creative Reaction Lab is building a youth-led, community-centered movement of a new type of civic leader.

AK

I believe this is an excellent opportunity to conclude our conversation on collaboration, partnership, non-extractive method-

NANCY GRAVES MAPS

ologies, and their implications. Upon reflection, I now understand that I sometimes failed to give back to the individuals who generously shared their insights with me during my research journey. This realization has made me ponder the importance of reciprocity and considering the impact of our work on the communities we engage with.

SM

There could be alternative approaches, such as gestures or establishing structures of partnership, that would enable us to minimize extractivism to the greatest extent possible. If we think about this on a longitudinal scale, we realize that we can only responsibly reciprocate later in our career, and it takes a while to build up to that. We have to be forgiving with ourselves.

fig. 6 Maskelyne DA Region of the Moon, 1972

Eric Robsky Huntley
&
Papers of Howard T Fisher

Liz Cormack & Eric Robsky Huntley

What was your entry point into the work that you're doing now?

ERIC ROBSKY HUNTLEY

I'm a child of the Rust Belt, and if you're a person who was more or less awake growing up in the Rust Belt, you were confronted in a very direct and obvious way with material disparities in urban life in a racialized and classed urban America. When I came out of my undergraduate program, in performing arts technology at the University of Michigan, I was less interested in the work I was doing in post-production for film than I was in the questions that were raised by some of the films I happened to be working on. I was around a lot of folks at that time who were engaging both critically and optimistically with the much trumpeted return of Detroit; there was a large group of people in and around Detroit working on trying to reckon with and rebuild in the wake of large-scale disinvestment, and I got pulled into those questions and got interested in my own upbringing and my own relationship to American urbanism.

LC

You've written about the geography department at the University of Michigan and lectured on the Laboratory for Computer Graphics and Spatial Analysis (LCGSA) at Harvard University.[1] What drew

Howard Fisher founded the Laboratory for Computer Graphics at the Harvard Graduate School of Design in 1965 to experiment with the potential of computer-generated maps. Supported by a large grant from the Ford Foundation, Fisher, who attended the GSD from 1926 to 1928 (although he received no degree), found Harvard more supportive of his academic appointment without an advanced degree than the Chicago institutions to which he initially appealed. ¡Spatial Analysis¡ was added to the lab's name two years later by the subsequent director, Bill Warntz. Known among historians of the field as ¡the Harvard Laboratory,¡ the lab is most famous today for its development of a range of tools and techniques that were incorporated into Geographic Information Systems (GIS).

you into these histories?

ERH

My PhD is in geography. I was a student of Matt Wilson, a geographer at the University of Kentucky. He was working on a book that drew on the archives of Howard Fisher, Bill Warntz, and Geoff Dutton, many of which remain unaccessioned in Harvard's special collections.[2] We fell in love with different parts of it.

Matthew Wilson is an associate professor of geography at the University of Kentucky and a visiting scholar at the Center for Geographic Analysis at Harvard University. He published *New Lines: Critical GIS and the Trouble of the Map* in 2017. Bill Warntz was the second director of the LCGSA. His arrival signaled a more permanent focus on geographical analysis as opposed to computer-aided architectural representation, which the lab had also explored under Fisher's direction. Geoffrey Dutton joined the lab as a research assistant while studying urban planning at the GSD and stayed on as a programmer until 1984. Among other innovations, Dutton created the first four-dimensional holographic cartographic display and developed the SEURAT program, which applied a pointillist approach to the display of cartographic terrain.

He was interested, ultimately, in the lab's pedagogy—how mapping teaches us to see, to pay attention, and to do both differently.

fig. 1 Contour mapping was one of the most widely used features of the SYMAP program, allowing users to visualize general trends in the data. These maps visualize year-over-year change in robberies from 1964 to 1966 in the Roxbury neighborhood of Boston.   *fig.* 2 This annotated map uses 1960 Chicago census data to instruct subscribers to the SYMAP correspondence course how to generate a contour map. By 1968, the correspondence course had provided introductory training via mail to over 500 users; subscribers would mail back their completed assignments for evaluation.

1

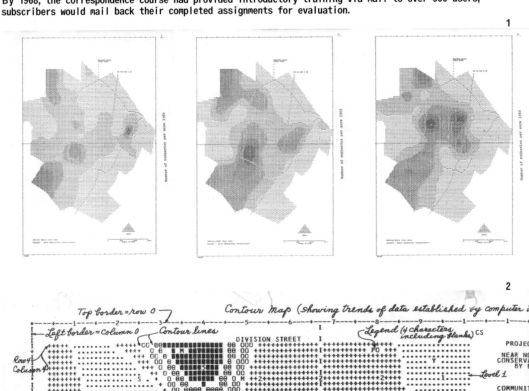

2

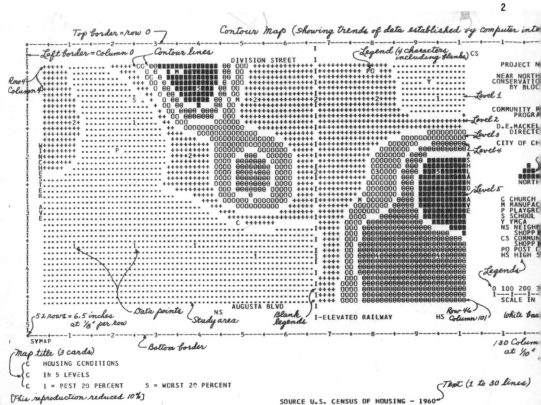

PAPERS OF HOWARD T. FISHER

I, on the other hand, fell for the extremely rich aesthetic and analytical vocabulary the LCGSA developed, the way they're doing cartography from different disciplinary backgrounds. The way that geography does cartography has always been a little boring to me: its tasteful Eduard Imhoff shaded relief; its nice, intelligible labels; its inoffensive serif fonts. And then I came across the lab's work, which, by those standards, is an affront: broken typewriters crudely piling ink on the page. And yet it's so much richer than what I think can be the kind of rote work of cartography as it shows up within my discipline.

LC

When reading Howard Fisher's writings, I was struck by the fact that the lab was founded for the exploration of computer graphics and only added spatial analysis a few years later. A lot of these early pioneers may have considered themselves to be artists as much as scientists. What was the lab's relationship to geography at that time?

ERH

That was Bill Warntz's innovation. Fisher was an architect. He was not a geographer. SYMAP, the program that generates many of these graphics, was developed by Fisher and Betty Benson. Benson was the programmer who built a lot of the infrastructure, but at that time, programming was feminized labor and therefore consistently undercompensated and underrecognized—see, for example, Mar Hicks's work.[3] Fisher was an architect, and he saw a

Mar Hicks, *Programmed Inequality: How Britain Discarded Women Technologists and Lost Its Edge in Computing* (Cambridge, MA: MIT Press, 2017).

presentation by Edgar Horwood at a conference in Chicago who was presenting some computer-generated cartography. Fisher essentially said, "Oh, I can do better than this." With Betty, he developed an application that was trying to put together a system to allow the individual to read the distribution of phenomena from the map, not just the statistical unit. Which one is this?

LC

This is a sample map they distributed as part of the training course for SYMAP.

ERH

Oh, yes, from the correspondence course. I think the obsession with contouring is really telling. They're looking at demographic data that's captured through the US census but visualizing it in a manner that's totally distinct from the way that a lot of folks even now tend to visualize it. They're not adhering to the measurement unit. They're saying, these measurement units are neither communicative of nor reflective of the underlying pattern. What is the pattern that we're observing? What is the actual distribution that we're observing? An undergraduate at the lab, Donald Shepard, developed an implementation of what we call an "inverse distance weighting algorithm," resulting in a famous 1968 paper.[4] Espe-

Donald Shepard, "A Two-Dimensional Interpolation Function for Irregularly-Spaced Data," from *Proceedings of the Association for Computing Machinery National Conference* (1968), 517–24.

cially after Bill Warntz comes, they're not that interested in producing visual representations as ends in themselves. They're asking questions about what we can understand differently about social space and what sits behind apparent phenomena. It's happening in a lot of parallel ways: there's a broad range of geographers who are trying to think about how to model social life using a range of metaphors drawn from physics. Bill Warntz is one of them. The visualization is never the result of an analysis. The visualization is part of the analysis. It takes its metaphors very seriously, and I always loved that.

LC

What kind of impact has that had on the way we do things today?

ERH

The inverse distance weighting method is something we still use today, but the lab's most direct and obvious contribution to the world of mapping as we know it is the fact that Jack Dangermond worked there as a graduate student.[5] Some of Esri's early code

Jack and Laura Dangermond cofounded Environmental Systems Research Institute (Esri) in 1969. Jack joined the LCGSA as a Masters student in Landscape Architecture at the GSD, where he used SYMAP to study and map air pollution in Los Angeles, among other work. Dangermond drew on techniques used at the lab to develop Esri's early GIS products, which are used by thousands of companies, universities, and most national governments today.

was functionally lifted directly from the LCGSA. This is also a culture of computing that's very different from the one we have now; strong proprietary relationships to your code base were quite a way off. The surprising thing about GIS is that it comes from outside the discipline of geography; its history has more to do with the LCGSA and state agencies. Suddenly in the 1980s, geographers were sort of confronted by it; the pressure started mounting on the discipline to engage, and it appeared as something from without instead of from within.

LC

I was just going to ask where you would place this kind of computing work in relation to planning. It was interesting that in Fisher's letters, there are all sorts of organizations—regional and city planning departments, police departments, the Federal Housing Administration, who are contacting the lab, asking for the software, expressing interest in starting to use their methods for

fig. 3 Completed as part of a housing study for the US Federal Housing Administration in 1967, these early examples of choropleth mapping use census data to show median income and percent change in population in New Haven, Connecticut. fig. 4 These pages from a 1967 Harvard Graduate School of Design Association publication promote the lab's evolution at the GSD. The left-hand page describes how to manually establish coordinates from a source map and transfer them to punch cards for use at Harvard's shared Computing Center.

3

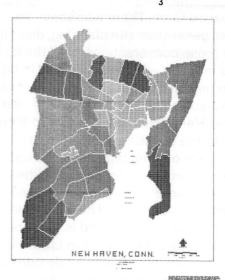

4

The recently-begun correspondence program is teaching the SYMAP technique to educators, city and regional planners, landscape architects, demographers, and geographers in this country and abroad. Helen Mansfield, Director of Publication, supervises preparation of every detail of the instructional materials, as well as evaluation and correction of the work the students return.

"Planning 7-3b. Computer Graphics: Theory and Application, Spring Term; Wed. 9-11. A seminar devoted to electronic procedures for storing, retrieving, and graphically displaying spatially disposed data of all kinds . . . Each student will gain practical experience through the application of computer technology to some research or professional problem of current interest to him, with group discussion of the particular methods he proposes to use and the results achieved." Professor Fisher leads discussion in his seminar. Students' projects encompass a wide range of locales and objectives: one is mapping housing conditions in Seoul, Korea, another is making an educational survey of Revere, Mass., and a two-man team is mapping abstract terrain to establish criteria for highway corridor selection.

THE TECHNIQUE

Making a computer map is a matter of a few simple steps. This student, preparing a map of Boston, first uses the manual digitizing board to establish the coordinates of the controlling points on the 'source map,' and enters the information on special coding forms.

Next he transfers the information from the coding forms to punch cards. The Laboratory is fortunate enough to have a keypunch in its offices. All other peripheral equipment, with the exception of the new electronic digitizer and the teletype, is at the Computing Center.

To have a record of his work in a form that is easy to check and store, the student lists his deck of cards. The machine reads the holes made in the cards by the keypunch and prints the corresponding characters on a special sheet. After listing his deck he will check the sheet against the coding forms to catch errors in keypunching.

quantitative analysis for planning work. How would you situate all that in the context of planning at the time?

ERH

At MIT, there were a lot of folks interested in computational methods in planning while harboring a certain amount of distrust toward them. There was some interest in generative methods, like generative site planning, and Fisher was present for some of those conversations, but I think planning has never really had its moment where it's gone all in on computation. Planning is strange in that it's an amalgam of practitioners: some urban designers, some social scientists. Jen Light has written a lot about this. Her book, *From Warfare to Welfare*, is lovely. She basically asks the question: how is it that in the 1960s and 1970s you have a bunch of think tanks that started as wartime operations suddenly consulting for municipalities on predictive computational work? There's a materialist analysis (after the war, Rand Corporation needed to find new revenue streams), but I think the long lesson from that period is that none of it worked. There were ambitious experiments in LA, in New York, where they were trying to implement large-scale computerized planning methods, but there was never any evidence that the work that came out of planning supported by computation was any better than the work that would've come out of planning not supported by computation. And indeed, there was some evidence that it was quite a lot worse.

LC

Why do you think that is?

ERH

My take on it amounts to this: the best reason to use computation for planning is also the reason it's never going to work. What you're always going to be assuming when you're trying to support planning work with computational methods is that provided we know something about how the world is, it's going to be evident what we should do. An "ought" falls out of an "is." And that's never true. It's never true that a description of the world is adequate to produce a revision to it. The term in philosophy is Hume's guillotine.[6]

In *A Treatise of Nature*, from 1739, Scottish philosopher David Hume put forth the thesis now known as Hume's guillotine, which states that a moral judgment cannot be made based on the facts alone. In other words, an "is, or is not" should not be confused with an "ought, or ought not."

LC

You co-wrote a textbook chapter on the ethics of GIS with Jeremy Crampton and E.C. Kaufman, is that right?

ERH

I did, yeah.

In it you share the work of the geographer and professor John Pickles, who says that increasingly with better technology, maps do more than just look, they control. I'm curious how you address that tension.

ERH

Broadly speaking, I was trained in what we call critical GIS, and the starting point for that subfield is that you're working with a technology that you're also trying to situate: you're taking GIS as both a subject and an object of study. Coming out of the 1970s into the 1980s you have quantitative geographers trained in early computational geography who started to realize that we can model until we pass out, but it's not going to change the world (David Harvey being the most famous among them).[7] And you had a

David Harvey, distinguished professor of anthropology and geography at the Graduate Center of the City University of New York, is a British Marxist economic geographer. In 1973, he published *Social Justice and the City*, which established him as the leading voice in the burgeoning field of critical geography.

bunch of human geographers who hadn't ever touched a computer making arguments about the abstracting and therefore violent nature of computation. One of my favorite pieces from this era is Nadine Sherman and Geraldine Pratt's essay "Care of the Subject: Feminism and Critiques of GIS." They say: look, we have to try to understand to what extent the broader social critique that we're bringing to bear on this set of technologies can be made using the language of the technology itself (and technologists themselves). It's really easy to confuse the marketing materials of a GIS company with the experience of doing GIS work. And the two things are deeply non-equivalent. I teach a lot with Catherine D'Ignazio at MIT who runs the Data + Feminism Lab and is the author, with Lauren Klein, of the 2020 book *Data Feminism*. There are few technologies more closely tied to colonialism and militarism than maps, and well, do methods have politics? Yes, they do. But does a method always fully carry its history with it? That's a meaningfully interesting and difficult question with no satisfying answer that doesn't depend almost entirely on the context of its use.

LC

During the Prospectors and Developers Association of Canada conference in Toronto, you and your collaborators worked to "unhide" what was happening on the convention center floor to reveal what this powerful group of mining interests was really doing at the conference. There's an interesting tension in GIS between the ability to surveil and the ability to uncover for liberatory ends.

fig. 5 The Teotihuacan Mapping Project, which mapped the location of pottery sherds to uncover the layout of the ancient city, was one of the first to use computer analysis in archeological research. This map shows the density of documented sherds per 10 square meters.

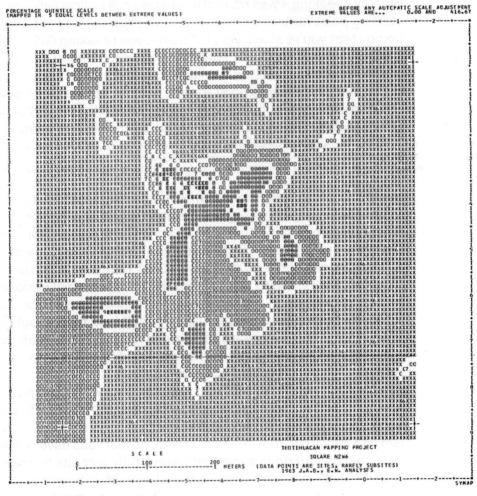

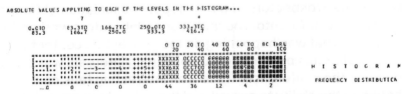

My response to that is what I call "mapping up." Recently, I've gotten into the work of a Berkeley anthropologist named Laura Nader, who was writing in the late 1960s and early 1970s. She writes really influentially about a pedagogical experiment she undertook with her students, responding to their dissatisfaction with the traditional anthropological approach. In general, as an anthropologist, the model was: travel to the colony, hang out for a while, come back to the metropole, and share what you found. What Nader's students—and Nader herself—said is, maybe we need to spend more time studying the colonizer than the colonized. Maybe instead of studying disinvested neighborhoods in American cities, we need to study the landlords and the mortgage lenders. Instead of studying people affected by the extractive industries who live next to tailing ponds, we need to go to Toronto and seriously examine the office cultures of the mining executives who are making those decisions. We need to understand these things as being produced by powerful institutions. Right now, I'm doing work on Massachusetts landlords in which we're trying to disentangle the housing insecurity industry. We've been looking at eviction filings and corporate records as they relate to property in Massachusetts, and we were struck by the percentage of eviction filings that are associated with the same few landlords. This is an enormous business. And again, it's not like this is intrinsically going to be more efficacious than another study discussing the problem of housing precarity or housing insecurity, but it feels a bit more…

It feels radical, a simple shift in perspective.

That's the hope. We put out a report last year with Homes for All Mass, which is a broad coalition of tenant organizers and housing advocates.[8] Massachusetts had a fairly meaningful eviction mor-

Eric Robsky Huntley, La-Brina Almeida, Shep Heaton, and Andrea Moon Park, "Housing Justice Beyond the Emergency: An Analysis of Racial Inequity in Eviction Filings Across Massachusetts," *Homes for All Massachusetts*, 2022.

atorium during the pandemic, at least for six months of it or so, and that moratorium lifted in October 2020. The question we were trying to answer was: what's the scene out there, what's happening? And a lot of the findings were distressingly predictable. If I ask you what you thought we'd find, you'd be right. Evictions happen disproportionately in communities of color. Poor folks and single mothers are having a really rough time out there. But also, a stronger predictor of eviction filing rates than any of these things is consolidation in the rental market and percent ownership by institutional landlords.

LC

Oh, wow.

ERH

I did an inventory of headlines that the report generated. Every single one just said that eviction filings disproportionately affect communities of color.

LC

Do you feel that shifts responsibility?

ERH

I feel like it absents responsibility. I feel like it treats an eviction as something that just happens. Like the weather. But someone files the paperwork; someone retains the lawyers. It's not just a naturally occurring thing. There are agents. I'm just really against any kind of analysis that excessively abstracts away the causal agent.

LC

You do a lot of work in education: you teach GIS and you're work-ing on youth education with the Boston Public Library at the Leventhal Map Center.[9] What is it that you wish everyone under-

The Norman B. Leventhal Map & Education Center was founded in 2004 at the Boston Public Library as a public-private partnership between the library and philanthropist Norman B. Leventhal. Its collection includes over 200,000 maps and 5,000 atlases dating from the 15th century to the present.

stood about this stuff?

ERH

Oh, that's interesting. I always get back to a couple of basic ma-terialist feminist things. I think a Donna Haraway-ism is that "maps are made but not made up."[10] I like that phrase because it suggests

Donna Haraway is an ecofeminist scholar and professor emerita in the History of Consciousness De-partment at the University of California, Santa Cruz. In 1980, she was the first tenured position in feminist theory in the United States. She argues that situated knowledge is about relationality, not relativism; as she states in a 2019 interview with the Los Angeles Review of Books, "facts are made in human historical circumstances, but not made up."

that people are making them, from their positions, for reasons, with intentions, with biases, with data that was itself the product of a huge amount of human labor. I always think about the US census. It's a basic thing in any GIS class, but that thing is the product of a titanic amount of human labor and is constructed using cate-gories that have radically changed. There's a wonderful graphic by the Pew Research Center that I like introducing students to. It's a timeline of racial categories used by the census over time.[11]

Pew Research Center, "What Census Calls Us: A Historical Timeline," 2020.

LC

I think I saw that at a Leventhal Map Center exhibit once.

ERH

And it's just an absolutely crystal clear demonstration that all of the categories we use are historical, they're all—

LC

—made.

ERH

They're all made. So very made. But then there's a tendency when you say that maps are made, knowledge is made, whatever it is that the takeaway can be: and therefore there is no ground. We're all drifting around in this world where we have no access to reality outside ourselves. The point that categories are made but not made up sums up my basic position, which is that everything is filtered through the institutions that make the things and produced by individuals with particular subject positions that have relationships to power. But that doesn't mean we have no ability to speak about the realities of the worlds that we inhabit.

LC

It's not a fiction.

ERH

It's not a fiction, it's an interpretation. It's one way in, it's one vantage point. It's something that you can look at from a range of different perspectives. I always show this image of a Geoff Dutton contribution to the lab, American Graph Fleeting. It's a hologram from the mid-1970s. This cylindrical glass enclosure, at about 18 inches wide, is sort of rotating, and it's showing the population density in the US over time. There's this photo of it that is so lovely. It's two people standing on opposite sides of this hologram. One person with a masculine gender expression, one with a feminine gender expression. And they're both looking at this thing with different faces. It's not saying the same thing to both of them. Yet the map is the same thing for both of them.

Kate Wagner & The Industrial Film Collection

Jennifer Li & Kate Wagner

JENNIFER LI
How's the University of Chicago?

KATE WAGNER

I'm teaching an undergraduate course in the art history depart-ment called "Sound and the Built Environment." It's about archi-tecture at the intersection of sound study and the history of science. We examine the built environment through listening tech-niques like experiencing soundscapes, deep listening, sound walks—practices that came into being in the 1970s, when the field of sound studies really became established. The point is to not rely on the primacy of the visual, which is a really difficult thing for art students to do.

JL

Are your students making soundscapes?

KW

Their main productive output here is a sound journal, which is about their interpretation of Chicago's urbanism. It's a blast discovering that the world is never actually quiet.

JL

Have you been to Public Records in New York City?[1] I visited,

Public Records is a sound room, café, restaurant, bar, and event space with the tagline "Exploring cul-ture through sound."

but just for a coffee. I didn't realize artists specifically seek out Public Records because of what it sounds like.

KW

There's a lecture in this class about the concept of high-fidelity, or "hi-fi." There's no such thing as a natural recording, so to speak; all recordings are simulacrums of events that happen physically in space. We talk about how the hi-fi technological language of the recording studio became commercialized for the listening room and also about concepts and aural simulacra created by stereo recording, which is kind of a psycho-acousti-cal trick. Artists would take artificial, electro-acoustical phe-nomena and imitate them in the physical world.

None of this is about McMansions![2] This is actually just what I studied in school.

McMansion Hell is Kate Wagner's popular biweekly satirical architecture blog that aims to educate the public about architectural concepts, urban planning, environmentalism, and history by spreading hate on the suburbs.

JL

Maybe with that we can get into the Industrial Film Collection. What did you think of the films?

KW

I have a kind of affection for industry as a subject in art, film, and architecture. When I was younger, I was really, really inter-

ested in socialist realism, but in an apolitical way. I was interested in the imagery of factories and the genesis of things we
use in everyday life. Industry is also a fascinating subject when
talking about architecture because of the kind of industrial
architecture that you see in these films. Reyner Banham wrote
A Concrete Atlantis about how daylit factories and grain silos influenced Walter Gropius and Le Corbusier.[3] But thinking about

Reyner Banham's *A Concrete Atlantis: U.S. Industrial Building and European Modern Architecture,
1900-1925*, originally published in 1986 by MIT Press, investigates striking architectural instances
wherein traits of the International Style are anticipated by industrial buildings in the United
States. Banham was an English architectural critic and writer widely known for *Theory and Design
in the First Machine Age*, first published in 1960.

industry as architecture is completely different, and I think this
is reflected in the films themselves, particularly the two devoted
to the construction and opening of steel plants in Japan.

JL

The films we've seen come from a collection gathered and produced by the Harvard Business School with the Harvard University Film Foundation to document the development of the industrial film genre. For some context, the Industrial Film Collection
includes more than 350 shorts dating from the 1940s to the 1980s.
They vary from instructional to narrative film to advertisement
and cover a number of topics including labor, motion, efficiency,
mechanization, industrialization, the relations of management
and workers, business policy, and administration. The three we're
discussing have to do with the industrial production of a common architectural element at a physical and structural scale. For
shorthand let's nickname them *America,* for *Steel Film of America*
(undated); *Nippon,* for *The Birth of a New Steelworks – Part III
Nipon Steel Corporation*, (undated); and *Yawatta,* for *Yawatta
Steel*, (undated).[4]

The Harvard Industrial Film Collection's titling is missing the second *p* in "Nippon."

KW

America is a film about unionization, about unemployment benefits that were part of a steel workers' campaign. This video is
from the perspective of a union toward a manager toward an employee, which is not a perspective that's commonly seen outside
of a boardroom. The other two films about steelmaking advertise
a firm's production techniques. *Nippon* is really almost a propa-
ganda film. All of the workers are depersonalized in a way. You
don't see the rhetorical language that you see in Art Deco frescoes
of these big, muscly workers with sweat dripping down their
faces. No, they're very neat, technical workers.

Right, they're shown to be parts of the steel factory itself.

They've depoliticized the workers completely in that film, whereas *Yawatta* depicts more of that masculinity, more of the violent physical processes that go into making steel. We, as people who study or work in architecture, are not the intended audience for these films. The intended audience is capitalists. These are interindustry videos. We're seeing industry from a perspective that we rarely see, which is really, really fascinating to me.

The opening shot of *Nippon* is of this huge, sprawling steel plant. If you open that up in a movie, people are like, "Oh, something bad is going to happen. These people are destroying the earth." Speaking as a member of the general public, industry feels inflicted upon us; it's not very comfortable to be around. A steel mill is a scary building. If you pass one, you think "Oh, I could die in there." It's sublime, I would say, in the Burkeian sense. It evokes pain and danger.[5]

In his 1757 treatise on aesthetics, *A Philosophical Enquiry into the Origin of Our Ideas of the Sublime and Beautiful*, Edmund Burke describes the "sublime" as grounded in pain and terror and therefore more powerful than pleasure.

I was going to ask you who you think the audience is, because I assumed that all three films were made for the general public as a means of recruitment. Essentially, "these are the tasks you'll be doing."

There are lots of shots in *Nippon* and *Yawatta* that zoom in on very specific parts of the steelmaking apparatus like, "Look at the quality of this particular part." I felt the films assumed that the people watching them had a specific knowledge of steelmaking and of the factory-building process, that the viewers would find value in the things that were highlighted. And of course, I don't know shit about steel, so I'm just like, "Yep, that is a nice pipe! That's a really cool chimney you got there!"

With these films, we're let into the secrets of production. The process of building a steel mill is interesting, how the parts come together. The other interesting thing is the ritual at the ends of *Nippon* and *Yawatta*, where they have a Shinto priest come in and bless the steel. It's almost like a combination of religion and Olympic torch lighting. I Googled, for example, "blessing of steel mills," to see if it translated across to America, and the results were mostly just ribbon-cutting ceremonies. So that's not very fun. If you can't sprinkle holy water on it, the end.

fig. 1 *America*, 01:45   fig. 2 *Nippon*, 16:32   fig. 3 *Nippon*, 08:49

JL

Run with a torch instead! That had to be one of my favorite scenes.

KW

In *Nippon*, my favorite scene was the transition shot from steel being formed with all the heavy machinery to then just panning up into the control room. I love that kind of stuff because building systems are interesting, but also aesthetically you have this really chaotic, hot, busy situation, and then you go into the sleek, minimal, cool control room. It's a great juxtaposition, a great vibe change.

I think my favorite scene in *Yawatta* is actually the guy who was heating the slugs—the rivets—and then slinging the hot rivets up to the guy who caught them in a giant mitt. That is so dangerous! I kept thinking, "Okay, that's sick. But also don't do that." The scene where they hoist the giant pipe and we scan up from the bottom of the steel mill to the top, and it's this big tower that's so architectural. This is a real finishing shot where you've seen these little processes, and they're finally topping out. It's so visceral from the very beginning. They start by dredging the body of water, which I'm guessing is the ocean. This whole film is about man's domination over nature, and it does not try to mediate that in any way.

JL

No birds flying across the water or tree planting at the end of *Yawatta*.

KW

You can see that self-consciousness in *Nippon*, though. The people who made that film tacked on that environmentalist crap at the end—I say "crap" because it's really contrived. You spent 30 minutes on this video about how you're building a steel plant, then at the very end, "But what about the birds?" It was such a juxtaposition that I literally laughed out loud when they started planting the trees.

JL

I was so surprised! I was thinking about when this film was made. There was a final diagram showing percentages labeled "Atmosphere" and "Earth"—what exactly were they measuring there?

KW

They're in hazmat suits digging into the ground like, "Oh, I know this is what environmental stewardship looks like in industrial settings, but it's a Superfund site."[6] I did a lot of research on Super-

"Superfund" is the colloquial term for the Comprehensive Environmental Response, Compensation and Liability Act of 1980 (CERCLA), which provides a federal "superfund" to clean up uncontrolled or abandoned hazardous waste sites that occur as a result of accidents, spills, and other emergency releases of contaminants and pollutants.

fund sites back in 2018 because I wrote about them in regard to ideas of landscape, how the Superfund site subverts this idea of natural and nonnatural places. Yet the horror comes from the knowledge of what really happens; there are no real aesthetic signifiers of the site after the remediation process. I visited a few remediated Superfund sites and found them legitimately terrifying. It's like they're haunted in a real way.

So I find the industry stuff in some ways scary. In other ways, it's beautifully architectural, almost like a Metabolist drawing, or when the steel mills' intricate piping evokes the Centre Pompidou. At the end of *Yawatta*, these huge, almost lithographs of steel are put in the bottom of the ocean and welded together. This whole thing is just so architectural, but it's different from an architecture that we know or practice, and that makes it foreign and scary. At the same time, we rely on these infrastructures for the things that make up our everyday life.

JL

I did some digging and found that Yawatta Steel Works was the first steelwork company in Japan and also a target for bombings in World War II. I realized after watching the films that steel factories were making weaponry at the same time. Nippon Steel was the product of a massive merger between Yawatta and Fuji Iron & Steel in 1970 and surpassed U.S. Steel as the world's largest steelmaker in 1975. So long after David J. McDonald was requesting unemployment benefits in *America*.[7] What do you think these

David J. McDonald was the president of the United Steelworkers of America (USW) from 1952 to 1965. After McDonald later lost the union's leadership, he retired to Palm Springs, though he stayed involved in unionization efforts until his passing in 1979.

films' motives are ultimately?

KW

I think the motive behind *America* is pretty obvious, which is to convince employers in the process of labor negotiations to consider these kinds of unemployment benefits. There's lots of rhetoric in that video that's just like, "All men want to work. We don't want to be bums sitting on unemployment like other people. We really do. We're good, hardworking Americans and not sus communists who just want a handout." That was pretty direct, on the nose. *America* is interesting to me in general because I work a lot with labor and architecture. Just hearing a union boss spell out what the benefits of a union are, even in a pleading way to an investor, is always relevant. I wish I had that plan for my job in the freelance writing factory.

The juxtaposition between *America* and the two other films was also important because *America* shows the steel worker

fig. 4 *Nippon*, 22:53   *fig.* 5 *Nippon*, 21:33   *fig.* 6 *Nippon*, 30:21

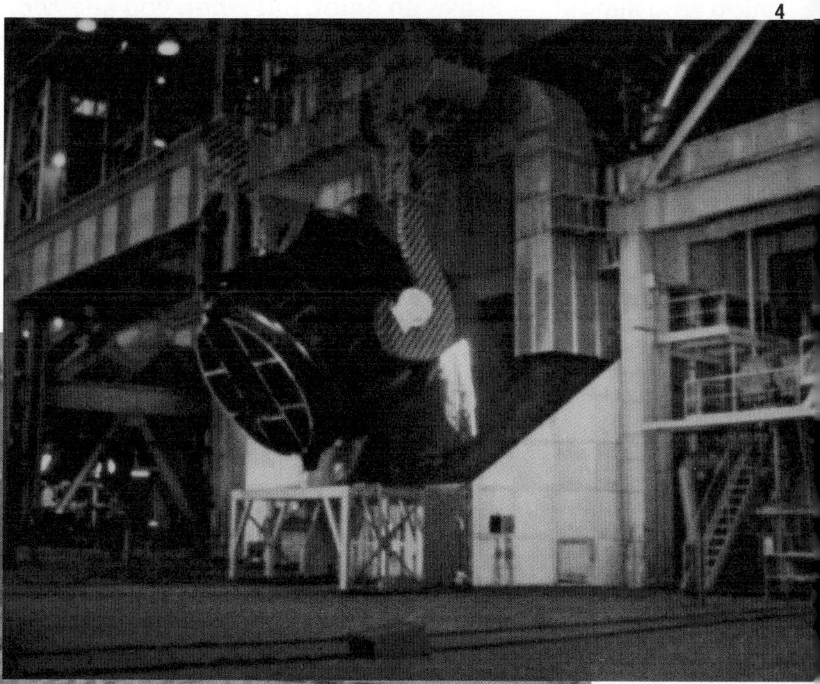

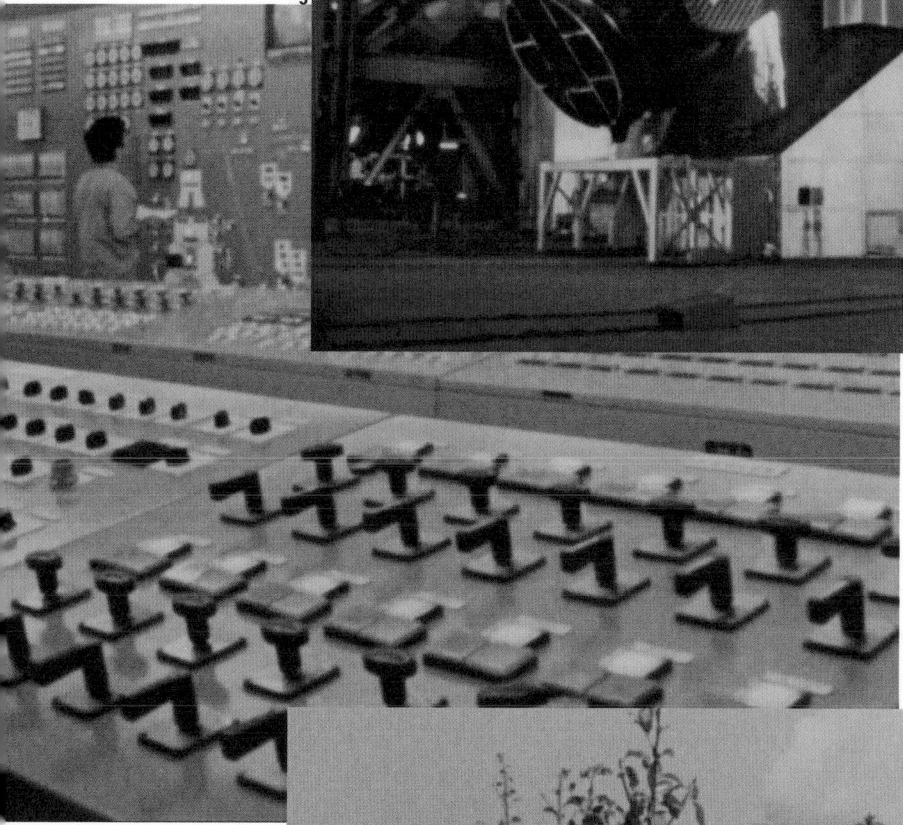

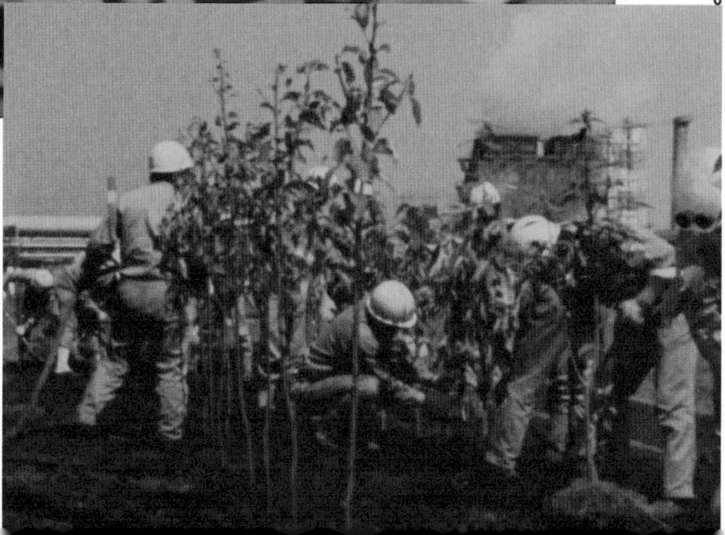

who's out of work. He's just some guy with a working class affectation who almost feels like an actor. But when you see *Nippon* and *Yawatta*, with people actually working in the steel mill, you're like, "Oh, that's a really hard job. That job is not a job I would personally want to do." Those were filmed in Japan by American production companies and assembled into silent films. I'm assuming that the intended consumers are American investors, either people who want to invest in the Japanese steel industry or steel companies considering purchasing land or investing in steel production in Japan. But the fact that they're American films has me believe that the audience is not necessarily Japanese.

JL

I was wondering why all the text was written in English instead of Japanese.

KW

At the end of *Nippon*, it just says, "Produced by a random American producer for the company." They commissioned this video in order to lure investors in some way or another.

JL

I thought of them as documentaries acting as advertisements.

KW

Yeah, exactly—it's like a document. That's true of a lot of industrial films, though. They document an industrial process but, in doing so, advertise that process, which seems contradictory to the documentary ethos. But as historical documents, they are some of the only glimpses we have into corporate thinking, industrial production, and investor logic. I have a friend in Slovenia who's also interested in this kind of stuff. We were watching a really fascinating documentary from the DuPont corporate archive about the process of making Freon and all of its potential uses for investors. Knowing what we know now about Freon, refrigerants, and their impact on the environment, it gives you the yips to watch that video.

The steel stuff, not so much. We still make steel. Steel is what most buildings are made out of, even now, whether through rebar or I-beams. Steel is still a really genuinely important part of architectural production. So even though the scenery and the factory are all sinister and scary and powerful and seemingly beyond human comprehension, the product that they make is not necessarily sinister. You know what I mean?

JL

Now I'm thinking of the diagrams that were inserted into *Nippon* and *Yawatta* to explain those apparatuses. One of the first diagrams in *Nippon* depicted the different mechanizations that went into making a steel slab. Later on in the film, maybe two-thirds of the way through, there's a diagram of data systems and what's recorded through each machine. We witnessed two stark ways of working: you're in all this heat and pounding, incessant water or you're in the calm control room, which is this specific tone of green. *Nippon* and *Yawatta* are silent films, but I felt that in both I could hear everything. In *America*, because the dialogue was so controlled, I actually felt I heard much less.

KW

I totally agree with that. If you look at the *Nippon* in the context of the 1970s, you're starting to see in the developed world the beginning of what people call "the managerial class": different stratifications of labor for managers versus workers that ultimately will accelerate with deindustrialization. From a historical perspective, seeing that stark juxtaposition really places that video in the 1970s.

You don't have that with *Yawatta*, which is really about heavy industry—lots of heat, lots of explosions, lots of really fantastical steelmaking shots, which I enjoy personally. It reminded me of *Koyaanisqatsi*, the 1982 antimodernist documentary with the Philip Glass soundtrack.[8] The soundtrack is like, "*Do! Do! Do!*

Koyaanisqatsi is a 1982 documentary directed by Godfrey Reggio that pioneered time-lapse filming techniques. Meant to showcase how life in the industrial world is out of balance in nature, its title draws from the Hopi word meaning "life out of balance."

Do!" But then it speeds through time: it opens with the Hopi reservation, this powerful, stark desert landscape; then the next scene is huge mining trucks with big streams of coal; then you're in the city; then you're in these neoliberal, neomodern, reflective skyscrapers from the 1980s; then you're in the computer. The pace of the movie increases and increases and increases, and this is supposed to represent how out of place we are with our origins, or whatever. That was a critical movie. These industrial films have footage of the same kind of processes but are in favor of these processes.

JL

My guess was that *Nippon* was produced post-1970, *America* in the 1950s, and *Yawatta* in the early 1900s.

KW

The 1970s felt very end-of-modernism: everyone was stuck in so many different crises, and the future looked extremely uncertain. You had guys like Sigfried Giedion, for example, looking backward at industrial modernity as some kind of high point of human achievement.[9] Meanwhile, postmodern architects were

In an email correspondence on labor and motion studies, Kate referred to Giedion's 1948 book *Mechanization Takes Command* as the "redheaded stepchild" of his writing expression ("That's an expression my mother uses. She was adopted and also redheaded, so that might be why."). Giedion is best known for his 1941 book *Space, Time, and Architecture. Mechanization Takes Command* relates the happenings of modern art and architecture to industrialization and mechanization.

looking at Pruitt-Igoe or modernism as a kind of failure. At the same time, you have the oil crisis, the start of deindustrialization, the start of neoliberalism, the environmental crisis. You saw all these apoplectic treatises like *The Limits to Growth*, for example.[10] You saw people living in earth houses. It just was a totally

The Limits to Growth is a nontechnical report published in 1972 on the possibility of exponential population and economic growth pointing toward environmental and economic collapse if "business as usual" were to continue.

batshit time.

I see so many parallels with the present. We've been living in the 1970s forever, except the problem is there was a transitional period between modernism and postmodernism then that we haven't had now. There's no clear artistic stylistic progression of architecture past—you can call it deconstructivism, neo-Modernism, or another "-ism," whatever Bjarke Ingels's and Zaha Hadid's buildings are doing. There really isn't a clear trajectory. The fundamental flaw with understanding architectural history as stylistic evolution is that there are many times where that isn't the case.

JL

I think that's a massive anxiety that exists right now in school and in the industry. At large corporate firms, let's say, they either reference themselves or they reference each other to produce new work. At school, I'll refer to the GSD, you're in such a large institution, you're able to pull from everywhere, regionally and theoretically. You could also be hyperintentional and navigate toward specific stylistic choices, but maybe it's not all stylistic.

KW

Well, it's all interconnected: alternative forms of practice, criticism, theory—like post-occupancy studies or maintenance studies, care studies, lots of stuff going on in theory that wasn't before. It's kind of the Bernie-era reintroduction of Marxism. There's always going to be a need for understanding the built environment in new ways.

I think for architecture, postmodernism is in the exact same trap as all the other arts. No one is going to be a Thomas Pynchon again, you know what I mean?[11] No one is going to do musical

Thomas Ruggles Pynchon Jr. is an American novelist. He won the US National Book Award for Fiction for his 1973 novel, *Gravity's Rainbow*.

minimalism again.

fig. 7 Yawatta, 04:08　　　fig. 8 Nippon, 28:37　　　fig. 9 Nippon, 26:12

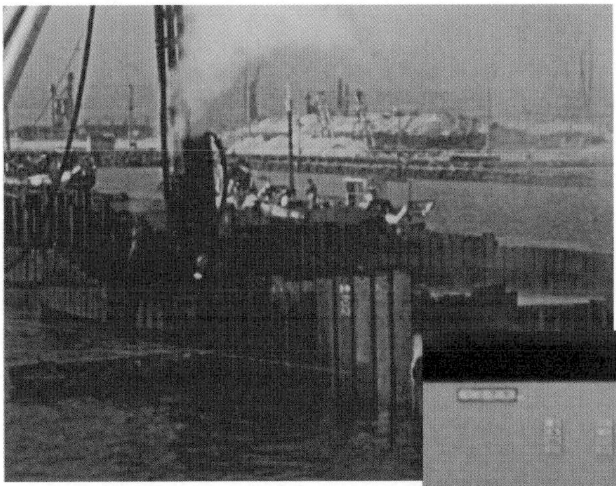

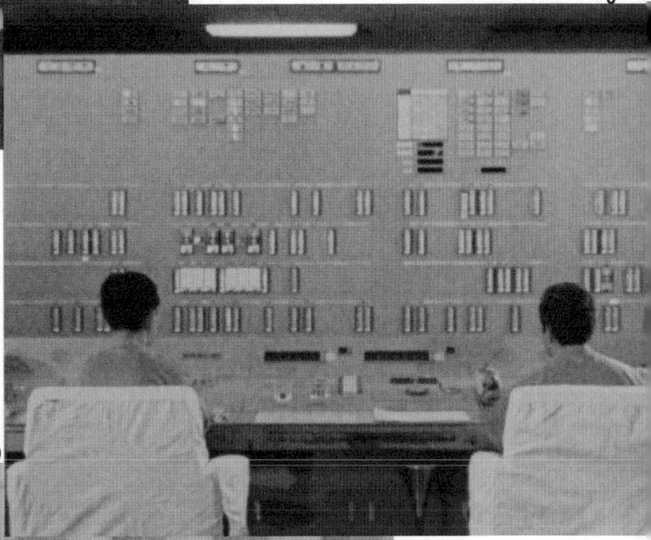

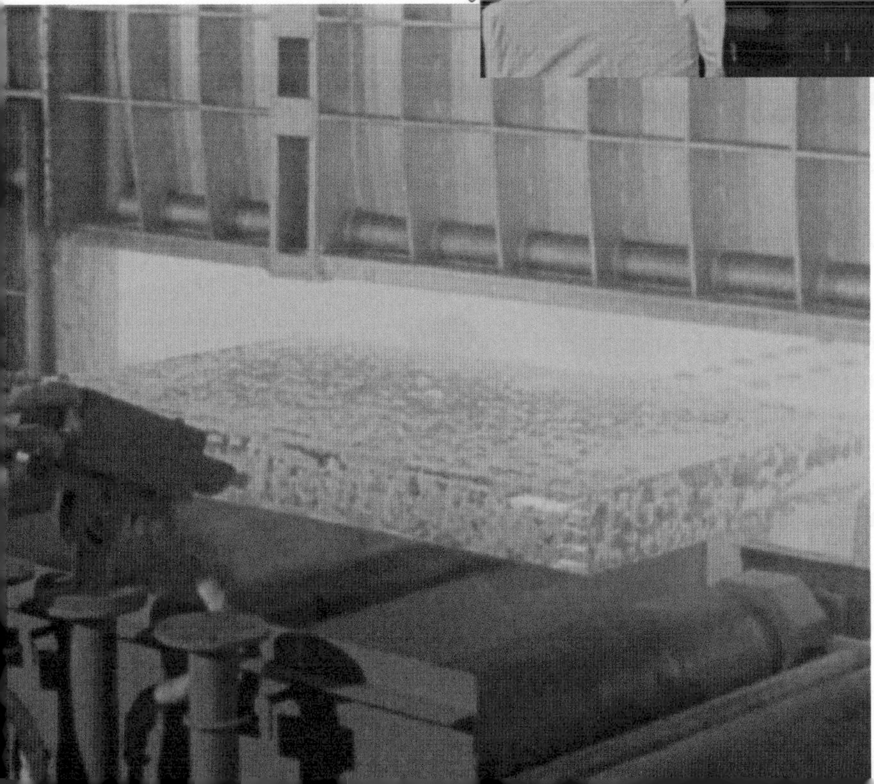

Musical minimalism?

That's Philip Glass or Steve Reich, they had different processes. Philip Glass uses this compositional technique called "additive process." He creates a single repetitive structure and then slowly adds to it, and every time he adds to it or changes it, it feels massive because the same structure or the same note or the same rhythm has just been relentlessly repeated for several minutes.

I'm thinking of hyperpop, which I assume is maximalism in music. There's so much noise going on simultaneously, so every time I listen to SOPHIE, for example, I might hear a different sound.[12]

Sophie Xeon was a Scottish music producer, songwriter, and DJ from Glasgow. She wrote and/or produced for Madonna, Nicki Minaj, Arca, Charli XCX, Kim Petras, Vince Staples, MØ, Camila Cabello, A.G. Cook, Diplo, and Shygirl, among others.

I think hyperpop is actually the first new musical idea that has happened in an extremely long time. I think the production techniques of hyperpop are our century's version of inventing tape music. It's majorly important for the development of music. I remember the first time I heard a 100 gecs song—I thought, "This is like listening to Xenakis, or something."[13] I was so excited when I

100 gecs is an American musical duo made up of Laura Les and Dylan Brady that has helped to define the genre of hyperpop. The duo self-released its debut album, *1000 gecs*, in 2019. Iannis Xenakis was a Romanian-born, Greek-French avant-garde music theorist, composer, architect, performance director, and engineer. Pioneering mathematical models in music, Xenakis was another major influence on the development of electronic music and integrated specific compositions into preexisting spaces.

first heard it. I was like, "Holy shit, this is so cool and so different and so unlike anything that has ever been made." When was the last time I felt that way about art, really?

I love that hyperpop bypasses the age-old drum-and-bass structure and instead creates atmosphere by layering textures.

Hyperpop takes techniques of record production, like auto-tune or remixing, and applies them in an equally distorted way to highlight the technique itself. It's a very virtuosic application of things that producers and DJs have been doing for a really long time.

These artists push technologies to their absolute limits and that, to me, is really extraordinary and experimental. It's also really popular, which gives me hope. We were just sick of the same shit for so long that now this really weird thing is really popular. My hope is that something similar will happen in architecture. We're tired of weird post-decon starchitecture projects. We're tired of the Vessel. We're tired of Rem Koolhaas.

fig. 10 *Nippon*, 16:13

Ryan W. Kennihan

&

Site of Reversible Destiny

Julia Spackman & Ryan W. Kennihan

After seeing these images of Yoro Park, are you convinced that architecture can reverse our mortal destinies? Either way, I hope these rainy photographs allow for a conversation about time and practice. What are your thoughts on these chaotically sliding couches? Does their existence remediate or intensify the bizarre nature of the park?

RYAN W. KENNIHAN

I wonder how meaningful a couch can be. I like specific responses to specific local conditions that engage universal problems. Furniture pieces can certainly do that, but perhaps a couch, a sink, or a bathtub is too general to engage these larger questions even through its misuse. It lacks a necessary charge gained through specificity, which allows us to read variations of morphology against a core definition.

JS

Would you say that artists Arakawa and Gins have neutralized "the weird" through its even application?

RWK

Even or not, I find shock value to be a problematic route to meaning. It's a Duchampian thing. They take a couch and embed it into a map of Tokyo. The other elements on-site are distracting because their design language is so personal—I feel it undermines that initial setup.

JS

I get that an overpowering style can be negative. Still, isn't it unavoidable? Even when an architect considers themselves to be only the medium of translation between craft and client, their decisions carry personality and inherent reference. Arakawa and Gins use loud colors and forms in their park in Yoro, but when they argue for immortality through a drastically different built environment, it is fitting.

RWK

It struck a negative chord with me, unfairly, since that was the type of work that was valued when I was in school. We all push against the zeitgeists of our elders, and I grew up in the rising starchitect era when personal artistry and novelty were of primary value. Whenever I see it now, I still have a negative reaction. Perhaps more productively, we can touch on the reliance on titling or written explanation in their work and what that says about legibility.

JS

Like in the case of Trajectory Membrane Gate, you're saying the title is unnecessary?

fig. 1 Kinesthetic Path   *fig.* 2 Trajectory Membrane Gate

2

SITE OF REVERSIBLE DESTINY

Just that it's overly didactic. I think that meaning comes to architecture through the inherently understood elements of daily life.

JS

Does that work beyond the scale of a private residence though? I understand you leverage familiar objects and contexts to arrive at meaning, but I feel like elements of didacticism are useful when designing for the public.

RWK

Instead of written words, I think resonance can be achieved through a proliferation of references. For example, at least in the European tradition, anything vaguely classical is understood. Whether we know it or not, whether we can differentiate Greek revival from Georgian, people know implicitly that public buildings of a certain scale in their city feel a certain way.

JS

That reasoning is distinctly postmodernist, no? Though the site opened in 1995, Arakawa and Gins seem to be operating with that same method of quoting elements.

RWK

Yes, but in this case their personal design language inhibits conceptual accessibility. I see curves, fragments of maps, and bright colors in these images. Though haphazard, these belong to the formal vocabulary of these designers. Their invented language, like all others, can be alienating. That's when titling becomes necessary and when meaning is described rather than felt. Are you a music fan, Julia? I'm going to bring up Kurt Cobain of Nirvana and Frank Black of the Pixies. Do you know either of these?

JS

Not The Pixies.

RWK

Kurt Cobain said he was just trying to write a Pixies song, and what came out was Nirvana. There is a difference between expression of self and formal inventiveness for its own sake. Architectural education at certain elite institutions over the past 20 years has tended to claim invention and ingenuity as primary objectives for architecture. I find it ethically questionable for architects to make a statement of novelty for themselves when working with the saved money of individuals.

JS

What about when the client enters the design process late or not at all, as in academic briefs? Is the projection of yourself onto the needs or desires of a future client problematic? Avoidable?

To answer, I'll bring up Howard David's study on the distance between those a building is for and those who make it.[1] In many

Howard David, *The Culture of Building* (Oxford: Oxford University Press, 2006).

cases, the architect is designing for a generic situation instead of
a specific person. The money might come from a consortium of
investors whose goals are complicated by those of the developer,
contractor, architect, local authority, fire people, and garbage
guys. In these hundreds of layers of competing objectives, the res-
ident is reduced to a buyer. I am privileged to get to respond
quite directly to things that are important to my clients. As for your
question about what to do when the client is missing, raw materials can inform the work greatly. Simply using everyday forms
and materials gives the design a material and formal language that
is accessible to people.

But you yourself don't strictly adhere to local methods. I've seen
some nods to Shinohara in your Baltrasna and Leagaun Houses.[2]

Kazuo Shinohara, House in White, 1966, Suginami Ward, Tokyo; Ryan W. Kennihan Architects, Baltrasna House, 2021, Dublin; Ryan W. Kennihan Architects, Leagaun House, 2014, Galway.

I have a little fun too, Julia. The external form is a material construction strategy, while the typological morphology is local.
Some of our current projects bring in super compositional and
formally plastic curves that are definitely not Irish. They are,
however, about light.

Speaking of light, why are all of the projects on your website
photographed in bright sunlight? This seems like the inverse of
the rainy images of Yoro Park's Site of Reversible Destiny, which
is typically photographed with bright colors and happy babies.

You'll have to come visit and see for yourself. The weather in
Ireland gets a bad rap. Yes, it's rainy, but it's also variable. It goes
from soulless gray to the most beautiful sunny day in ten minutes.
We have a very high summer sun and a very low winter sun that
only rises 13 degrees above the horizon.

How would you say the sensibilities of the thoughtful houses
you've designed translate to larger buildings or expressions?
You'll have to forgive my insistence on scale. I've mostly worked
on massive urban developments and am hungry to think
through something smaller.

SITE OF REVERSIBLE DESTINY

fig. 3 Reversible Density Office   *fig.* 4 Kinesthetic Path

The opportunity to engage with your own interests is difficult, especially at this stage in your career. I would begin by asking what things you want to build and then chase after where that's possible. I did that and ended up in Ireland. Immediately when I came here, the office I worked at handed me a house project. My colleagues were busy, and since I didn't know anything about construction, I just asked the lads at the site what they would do. I got my start by using the most basic solution and tweaking it into something special.

You leveraged naivety in the beginning. Do you still put that hat on?

Although I've been intimately involved with buildings for 20 years, I still very much know what I don't know. I understand that the builders have immense expertise and I do not lord over anything. David Pye, the designer-craftsman and teacher at the Royal College of Art in London, wrote on this topic.[3] He details the limi-

David Pye, *The Nature and Art of Workmanship* (London: Herbert Press, 1968).

tations of the designer and describes the ineffectiveness of even the most exquisite and complete details without the person there with the knowledge, skills, and dexterity to make the thing.

There's tweaking of conventional details and tweaking of existing buildings. I'd like to discuss the latter, especially as this relates to newer, nonhistorical stock that's built cheaply. I know you have some experience there, can you tell me about it?

When we work with older protected structures, there's a very obvious significance. Extensions from the 1960s with leaking roofs are less clear. We get quite a lot of houses from the 1970s and 1980s that perform terribly environmentally but have value in the embodied energy of their structures and concrete footprints. Many of our projects have a 1980s bungalow building buried within somewhere. The roof of our Beach Road House, for example, gets both its height and pitch from the 1990s building at its core. In these cases, we use energy and weathering upgrades to give a new aesthetic life to the structure. Insulation in particular gives us reason to change window shapes, because we need to insulate the sides of the openings.

When you mention the 1980s, I immediately think of laminate windows. What happens to the plastic composites that are so common in buildings of this era? Can you reuse them at all?

SITE OF REVERSIBLE DESTINY

fig. 5 Geographical Ghost

fig. 6 Site of Reversible Destiny

SITE OF REVERSIBLE DESTINY

Reuse requires a lot of research and realism regarding the constraints. We build in masonry, as opposed to timber, but there's a big difference between lime and concrete mortar construction. In terms of reuse, with lime, we can disassemble the bricks. But with cement, there's very little we can do with it, other than make rubble for foundations. The degradation of materials over time also adds difficulty. An engineer won't work with roof trusses rotted by the moisture in the west of Ireland.

JS

Does reuse ever become an insurance nightmare on these smaller houses?

RWK

Not as bad as in the States. We got a small taste of American insurance policies when contributing to the Chicago Biennial. We spent weeks talking through the piece's arrival and transport. Whose insurance takes it from the plane to the truck, and whose insurance takes it from the truck to the loading dock, and while it's sitting in the loading dock, whose insurance is looking after it? Who's responsible for the people that carry it up the elevator? Who's unloading the packages? Here, the guys will take it off the truck, drop it off, unpack it, and throw out the packages without discussion.

JS

I see the difference! You mentioned people won't approve completely rotted things, but it does seem like there's some creative flexibility or at least open-mindedness to breaking the new material standard. Why is that?

RWK

The culture is open to slightly risky things. Though the permitting apparatus is highly subjective, it values the existing context, which improves the built environment, and it recognizes the value of employing architects. This is reflected in popular media, too. Your average person would come in contact with the best architects in the country because they would be in the paper, not in the art section but in the property section. This positions our work as useful and valuable to everyday culture.

JS

In a weird way this gets at architectural representation. The ways in which buildings are described and shared beyond their image says a lot about culture. In my own experience, design was professionally expressed to clients best through a cost projection spreadsheet. In your case, the engagement with architecture in the daily newspaper must also be related to a smaller scale

8

9

SITE OF REVERSIBLE DESTINY

financing structure. Are the desires of everyday clients really able to drive creative solutions?

RWK

There's less of a financial disincentive because if you break standard it'll cost only a little more. That means design is still in reach of everyday people. If you want to practice in the States, you'll need a deep understanding of the most ordinary things to avoid the insurance necessary for custom work. But if you know the products and people well enough, architecture for everyone just might be possible.

Fernanda Canales & Harvardevens Village Photographs

Emily Hsee & Fernanda Canales

fig. 1 Aerial view of Harvardevens Village after its conversion from an army base with military hospitals.

EMILY HSEE

Let's jump right into these images of Harvardevens Village, which was a self-contained community established by Harvard in 1946 to provide housing for married World War II veterans attending the university. Postwar housing policies and ideology have influenced so much of our understanding of housing in the United States, so I'd love to talk about what this strange village can reveal about the current perceptions and possibilities of housing.

FERNANDA CANALES

Harvardevens Village exemplifies very clearly the transitions of ideals from that era to the present day. It reflects the evolution of public programs and the public's awareness of housing, not just as it pertains to private institutions like Harvard but also in terms of government involvement and federal funding. It exemplifies a commitment between private and public institutions, the government, and society's interest in housing war veterans and students, with the aim of improving society through housing. But then, with the fall of support for the village, we witness housing becoming the individual's problem. There is no longer a concern for students and their families, the relationship between living and working, transportation, socializing, and addressing health issues.

EH

Harvardevens was originally an army base with military hospitals, which the university converted to provide housing, social activities, and support for its residents over a three-year period. The property returned to the army in 1949. It's worth noting that the postwar national housing crisis was followed by significant federal support, including GI bills, which made projects like Harvardevens possible. But Harvardevens was built to house Harvard students specifically, so I want to start by talking about the relationship between these public programs and elite private institutions.

FC

How a society is housed is how a society is constructed. When we leave housing completely in the hands of individuals and the development of market-driven economies, we stop considering housing as a community. We stop considering the relation between the city and the house. Harvardevens Village didn't only consider the housing unit, but also included recreational facilities, infirmaries, barber shops, parlors, and even a grocery store. It was intended to be a cooperative, in a larger sense of the word. It wasn't just about neighbors sleeping side by side but rather building a system for society to function as a whole. It addressed the question of how houses were going to be related to educational, recreational, and social considerations.

This detachment between the house and the city, which started to occur in the decades after the postwar period, exemplifies the disconnect between people, their workplaces, and society, including access to resources. Harvardevens was quite far from Harvard, so the commute time was a huge issue. Train schedules had to align with the logistics of students' lives and their daily activities, such as getting food or going to the library, exemplifying a concern that was important at the time. At universities today, there is much less thought given to how students arrive on campus, the relationship between the students and their families, or the availability of childcare facilities and other related concerns. This lack of care, of course, also extends to teachers and various staff members who take care of the university.

EH

That's interesting. I had seen Harvardevens as the government potentially shifting its responsibility to house people to a powerful private institution. But your interpretation is that the collaboration itself actually exemplifies a time when housing was given more importance because multiple actors—both public and private—were invested in housing?

FC

Exactly. It also touches on other considerations such as the temporality and reuse of buildings. When the government had an army hospital that was no longer used after the war, who took the initiative to ask what to do with the existing infrastructure? Was there another institution that could find usefulness in the program? How could the adjacent railroad be used? Establishing connections between existing infrastructure, such as warehouses or railroads, requires effective communication among many different actors. The fact that this project involved action and responsibility from the government, from a private institution, as well as from the students, reflects the interests of the time. It wasn't merely about individual choices; it addressed the future of society and the city in a more complete sense.

EH

That makes sense, but it's also an optimistic view of the collaborative nature between public and private actors. I was looking into the specific legal relationship between the government and Harvard, and as far as I can tell, the federal government authorized the housing to Harvard, but Harvard still managed and funded it. This created an uncertain and ambiguous private–public relationship, which Harvard used to its advantage in order to avoid paying local taxes. This also meant that there was no legal authority or enforcement within the village, and therefore no one inside could be arrested. While the incentive of not paying taxes is clear, it raises an interesting question about trust. In the US today, public housing is very heavily surveilled and policed. I'm curious to hear your thoughts on whether the fact that the residents were specifically Harvard students played a role in this dynamic, or if it was more influenced by the broader context of the postwar era.

FC

I was surprised to learn that there was a guarded gate equipped with a gun as the single entry point to the village. It reflects the potential danger and problematic relationship between housing and public space, as housing projects have often been designed as "ghettos" or places that accentuate segregation. The way we have responded to that by further restricting access with fences, guards, and impossible mortgages actually works against the intention of creating safer spaces.

If you break down walls, invite people in, and blur the divisions between inside and outside, as well as public and private spaces, the spaces actually become safer. This is an important lesson that is now clear in the 21st century. It also has to do with not identifying a sole user group. Harvardevens provided houses exclusively for married veterans, so the village generally lacked diversity in age and activity. The limited range of activities led to more conflicts than if it had been more open and diverse. For example, while there were babies in the village, there were no older children, and consequently, certain spaces remained empty during certain times. When we fail to relate housing to real-life diversity, when we exclude teenagers, the elderly, people with different interests, or people who actually work there, buildings become useless. They accentuate the existence of an idealized prototype user, rather than reflecting the reality of society and addressing diverse users' needs.

EH

What you're saying about physically opening up space and blurring the boundaries between inside and outside to enhance safety also reminds me of Jane Jacobs's concept of "eyes on the street."[1] It feels so simple and obvious that visual openness,

Coined by urbanist Jane Jacobs, the "eyes on the street" concept emphasizes the importance of visual openness and community interactions in enhancing safety within urban spaces. It underscores the idea that increased visibility and social engagement contribute to a more secure and vibrant environment.

being able to hear, and generally having more interactions on different scales and layers can contribute to a safer and more robust community. Yet there is a common misconception that seclusion equals safety, particularly in closed-off, wealthy neighborhoods.

FC

You can understand how ingrained the idea of seclusion is today if you examine the American dream house. There is an emphasis on single-family dwellings and private cars, producing a type of housing that is detached from public transportation and the cooperative principles of garden cities proposed by Ebenezer Howard.[2]

The concept of "garden cities," put forth by Ebenezer Howard in the late 19th and early 20th centuries, gained popularity as a vision for planned communities that blended urban conveniences with countryside living. Howard promoted satellite communities that surrounded the central city with greenbelts in between. These garden cities aimed to address the social and environmental challenges of urbanization by ensuring each city contained a certain proportion of residences, industry, and agriculture.

For me, an exhibition called "Tomorrow's Small House" at MOMA, curated by Elizabeth Bauer Mock, makes very visible the shift from a more collective attitude toward housing to an individual one.[3] The exhibition took place a couple of months prior to the

The "Tomorrow's Small House" exhibition, curated by Elizabeth Bauer Mock at MOMA in 1945 showcased architectural models of proposed homes from up-and-coming architects of the time.

end of World War II, at a time when people in the US were preparing to build one million new houses each year, along with extensive remodeling of existing housing. The exhibition explored how to achieve this quickly and affordably, considering time and financial constraints. Only one of the nine models presented in the exhibition (of houses designed by architects such as Frank Lloyd Wright and Philip Johnson) showcased a collaborative housing project centered on the importance of the relationship between the house and its neighborhood.

In the 1940s, well-being meant survival and efficiency. Later, it became associated with spending money and acquiring consumer goods, tied to the consumption-driven economy centered around single-family dwellings, cars, TVs, and domestic appliances. The magazine *Arts & Architecture*, under the direction of John Entenza, played a significant role in this transformation.[4]

Arts & Architecture magazine, which ran from 1929 to 1967, was an American architecture, design, landscape, and art magazine. It played a crucial role in shaping architectural trends and facilitating conversations about design, including its renowned Case Study House program, which explored experimental and affordable dwelling concepts.

In 1943, Entenza launched a building competition that focused on small and affordable houses, around 100 square meters on average, and then initiated the Case Study House program in 1945. In the 1960s, when Entenza left the magazine, the Case Study Houses, which aimed to encourage prefab construction, emphasizing affordability and efficiency, were three times that size,

fig. 2 Harvardevens Village swimming pool in 1947.   *fig.* 3 Nursery school with a generic balloon frame structure in 1947.

2

HARVARDEVENS VILLAGE PHOTOGRAPHS

with pools and double-height ceilings. The logic of industrialization had just become an aesthetic.

This transition between ideals is exemplified very clearly in the images of the Harvardevens project. The images of the housing and the interiors are almost soldier-like: everything is focused on essential needs and reproductive economy. When you see the images of the people playing outside by the pool, doing recreational activities, it strikes you how opposite those two worlds are. The interior world represents a private, rational, and even lonely space where you basically only sleep and cook. Well-being, playfulness, and leisure occur on the outside. It's even hard to imagine that the people who are in the pool are the same ones we are looking at inhabiting the houses. It seems completely disconnected, as if we were seeing two different societies. The ambivalence portrayed in the images makes visible the shift from times of war and scarcity to a more consumer-driven and capitalist society. The duality is exemplified by a disconnect between the interior and the exterior, between architecture and the world.

EH

I like the framing of the village as a place with inherent contradictions. I noticed this too with the role of patriotism and Americanness in these photos. The shared space and collectivity outside of the home, such as the shared backyard, pool, and nursery school, contrasts with what we might view now as the typical American home. But then there's an American flag, it's sited on a military base, and it's legally and physically independent from its surroundings, which also feels quite American to me.

FC

Another American housing concept is the historical balloon frame structure.[5] In 2021, the US Pavilion at the Venice Biennale high-

The balloon frame structure, a distinctive construction method in American architectural history, uses vertical studs and horizontal members to create a lightweight and efficient framework.

lighted this American construction method, which was reinterpreted throughout the years, for example, in Frank Lloyd Wright's 1915 ready-cut system, in which he patented hundreds of houses based on standardized precut timber. It was a solution not only for housing but for any building typology. Harvardevens, for example, was so generic, just an abstract standardized framework, that you wouldn't even be able to guess its original typology as a hospital.

When Frank Lloyd Wright or Rudolph Schindler conceptualized how the balloon frame could be used in the early 20th century, they saw potential in the system's inherent flexibility. The balloon frame is actually similar to traditional Japanese timber building methods that allow for communication between the inside and the outside and for spaces to transform throughout different seasons or even within the same day. It's striking that just decades after the balloon frame system started to be used in the US, it lost this adaptable potential. It became a single solution. This was already the case when Harvardevens was established. As you can see in the images, the structure does not allow for personal adjustments or different living configurations.

The photograph of the kitchen shows its efficiency, but the space doesn't account for ideas of collectivity or communality that domestic scientists such as Catharine Beecher, Ellen Swallow Richards, and Melusina Fay Peirce had developed.[6]

Catharine Beecher, Ellen Swallow Richards, and Melusina Fay Peirce were American feminists and educators who in the 19th century contributed significantly to the discourse on domestic architecture and women's roles in shaping the built environment.

These women showed the advantages of not just making kitchens more efficient but also making a place to collectivize services and consequently liberate the burden of domestic labor. There was a way for efficiency and improvisation to coexist. So it's striking to see that in a housing project of 400 units for students with wives there was no attempt to introduce those great developments.

EH

It seems like we're talking about two types of housing: one in which the home offers only the bare minimum, and life predominantly happens outside of it, and another extreme in which the single-family home encapsulates everything, leaving little room for activities outside its confines. However, what seems to be missing is a third type of housing where the division between the home and the outside is not so defined.

FC

What's impossible to understand is that this missing third type was already there. These domestic reformers, including Charlotte Perkins Gilman, were from Boston.[7] If they had still been alive

Charlotte Perkins Gilman was a notable feminist and sociologist in the late 19th and early 20th centuries. Her writings examined women's roles, gender equality, and domestic space.

in the 1940s, I'm sure they would have had a lot to say about projects like Harvardevens. Given that the people living there had very similar schedules for eating, studying and washing clothes, it would have been really easy to convert this housing project into an example of living efficiently and collectively.

In postwar economies, the priority was to do everything cheaply and quickly. It doesn't make any sense that for every, say, 100 families living there, you would need 100 refrigerators, 100 stoves,

HARVARDEVENS VILLAGE PHOTOGRAPHS

fig. 4 Apartment kitchen equipped with refrigerator, radiator, and sink, ca. 1947–49.

and 100 vacuum cleaners. Think about the redundancy not only of the appliances but also of the time spent on domestic labor. We're not just speaking about the things you buy but the hours and resources you spend on the same few things: food, clean clothes, waste water. It's amazing that Harvardevens didn't take advantage of the potential of collectivizing services and domestic labor. And it's amazing that we're still not developing those ideas further today.

So, we can learn a lot from this project, particularly its radical cooperative potential.

EH

Absolutely. Projects from this era could have been such an important turning point toward more collective living. But in Harvardevens there was a very conservative idea of what the family was and who the residents were: the male veteran Harvard student with a wife and a young child.

Despite that, and despite the rigid architecture, you start to see a growing sense of communal life. It's a shame that this could have been an important case study for what housing could be, but instead it took a very different turn.

FC

Completely. Some of these images look like cooperative housing projects in Sweden, or West Germany, or many places in Europe at the time, but without the social agenda. And there was the intention to have a grocery store at this project, a bowling alley, a theater, and barber shops. There were houses with one, two, and three bedrooms. Despite the homogeneity of the inhabitants, there was some recognition of diversity and the need to link this community with a real city. But, of course, there's a gap between these minor attempts to make this community self-sufficient and the potential that the domestic reformers saw in cooperative living.

EH

On a slightly different note—this is a personal interest of mine— is the idea of homemaking at a former site of war and violence. That's something I explored when I was in your studio. Harvardevens is a fascinating example, because families were living inside of the hospitals where, previously, injured people were potentially dying. There's a lot of violence embedded in the site. How do those legacies transfer within the home?

FC

Buckminster Fuller's Dymaxion Deployment Unit, later renamed the Defense House, comes to mind.[8] It was promoted as a shelter

The Dymaxion Deployment Unit was designed in 1940 and aimed to provide a flexible and efficient housing solution through its modular and transportable design. They were manufactured in the early 1940s and deployed all around the world as a solution to wartime housing needs.

in war and a beach house in peacetime. How to transition from war to peace was a significant question at the time. War, earthquakes, pandemics—these traumas are embedded in the history of our cities. Architecture and buildings are the most visible or tangible recipients of memories in cities. They take on a role of accommodating, for example, the transformation of a church from a place of rituals into a space for refugees. Many typologies— churches, stadiums, schools—can take on that ambivalent shift in times of emergency because of their size or public condition. I'm always amazed that we can transform spaces that have a very fixed, iconic image or a determined role in society. These images that we see of 1946 are very close to images that I've seen of Mexico City's earthquakes as recently as 2017, border cities with immigration, the current war in Ukraine, or the pandemic. In all instances, we expect architecture to have that role in accommodating different uses and serving as a caring space, a welcoming place that supports inhabitants in different ways throughout history. That is why I find it questionable when architecture is too specialized, because we know that buildings endure more than their current functional programs.

Buildings that are meant only for one thing are problematic: residential buildings meant only to sleep, office spaces that are now vacant, or buildings in which you can do only one task. We know life is not like that, our activities are never just one-sided. Buildings are much more interesting when they do more things, and these images of Harvardevens are so relevant because people are finding ways to do those activities despite the fixed architecture.

For me, Harvardevens Village is a project that attempted to function as a bridge, for example, by linking an abandoned infrastructure with existing housing needs, a vacant faraway plot with the urban reality of the university, or family life with individual needs. It's a project that established a way to unite the communal and the private and give new life to unused infrastructure. If we had more projects that build bridges instead of accentuating divisions, we would definitely not be speaking about cities with buildings but rather about cities with communities.

Yasmeen Lari & Mimar

Syeda Aimen Fatima & Yasmeen Lari

fig. 1 *Mimar* 1

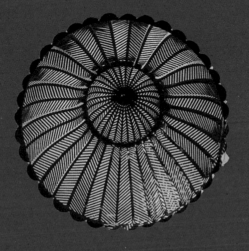

MIMAR 1·1981

SYEDA AIMEN FATIMA

Let's start by talking about *Mimar: Architecture in Development*, an international architecture journal that ran from 1981 to 1992. According to the magazine's editor, Hasan-Uddin Khan, the unique cutout covers were inspired by Mughal miniatures. These minuscule paintings were known for "providing a window to a world," just as *Mimar*'s objective was to provide a window into the world of non-Western design.[1] How do you remember the journal?

Mughal miniatures are small paintings measuring only a few square inches that often illustrate manuscripts and art books from the 16th and early 17th centuries. The style derives from both Persian and Indian techniques dating back to the 9th century and takes its name from the Mughal Empire, which was established in 1526. Even at their small scale, the paintings are extremely colorful and precise, and some details were added using brushes with a single hair.

YASMEEN LARI

It was a very good effort, and they did a commendable job of highlighting a lot of people that were not widely known. So, in a way *Mimar* served its purpose. Khan gathered a very high-powered team, and they produced the journal with a great deal of care.

SAF

It was a very valuable point of reference for people interested in the built environment and in the developing world before the time of the internet. Professor Khan has said, "Even after all these years, I feel there is still the need for an international periodical … that has a point of view and could be a champion for new causes, from that of the vernacular and indigenous building to high-tech design and sustainability."[2] What do you think is the role of such

Hasan-Uddin Khan, "Developing Discourses on Architecture: The Aga Khan Award for Architecture, the Journal *Mimar: Architecture in Development*, and Other Adventures," *Journal of Architectural Education* 63, no. 2 (2010): 82.

discourses in the world of design, considering the internet as a resource today?

YL

On the one hand, for most architects, it was good to know that there was a focus on the Islamic world. On the other hand, most of the time it was promoting "starchitect" culture, which at that time seemed valuable. But I think a lot of focus should have been on poverty and other issues that were not often taken up.

Most architects are not sensitive to situations in the developing world, the Global South, and the Islamic world, which have totally evolved due to climate change. There are so many disparities in the world now: poverty levels are high, and architects do very little to help those in need. These glossy high-tech publications were only accessible to people who could afford them. Today of course, with the internet, access has changed. But I think the focus of these publications must also change.

Mimar had correspondents from all over the developing world. In your mind, how important is it who writes about these subjects? What is the relationship between the architect and the journalist?

I don't know the role of the journal or the journalist today, to tell you the truth. The world is open now; there are many other media to use. I would really like to see a special emphasis on women's capabilities. It's rarely acknowledged that women possess certain skills that are valuable in leading teams for rehabilitation or construction. The role of women in the work that I do, for instance, has rarely been acknowledged. It doesn't have to be by journalists anymore; it can be anybody.

Mimar's second issue, in which you were featured, highlighted women in the built environment and discussed how women's roles in systems of production were neglected even then. Many people in the developing world are now able to create their own platforms and can transmit information to the world outside of the journal format, for example, by maintaining a YouTube channel that documents the work you're doing.

Creating a digital platform for knowledge is one of my goals during my upcoming professorship at Cambridge University. I said that whatever they would have paid me should go towards supporting student research in Pakistan. We need to have these kinds of platforms for people who want that knowledge, and to have this information available.

I have been very grateful for all the attention that's been given to my work. But the time has come for us to look beyond glossy pictures at the philosophical basis of various issues and ask, "What is it that we really need to do in today's world?" Of course, I've done my share of designing beautiful buildings, but I also know that kind of work has no relevance today. In the 1980s the world was our oyster! You could do what you wanted to do; everything seemed possible. But the world is different now, with so many disasters, with climate change. We know how our designs wreak havoc on the environment. Almost forty percent of all carbon emissions are because of the way architects and engineers are building today.[3]

In June 2022, *The Economist* reported that buildings and construction are responsible for almost forty percent of all energy-related carbon emissions. This includes both operational and "embodied" carbon in buildings. "The construction industry remains horribly climate-unfriendly," *The Economist*, June 15, 2022.

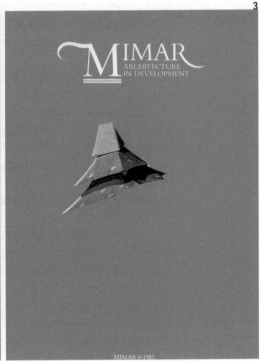

There are certain materials that can counteract the current emissions. So, why aren't architects looking into that? Because it's not dramatic? Because it won't produce something that will be impressive or iconic? Because it's not good for our ego? Because it won't appear in a glossy magazine? If I put up an iconic structure in the 1980s, well, what value does it have anymore? It is not doing anything to help people rise above their own impoverished conditions.

There are so many issues that one needs to be considering when creating something. How is it impacting communities? How does it affect those who pass your beautiful building? Is it of value to people with difficult lives who walk by it on the street in Pakistan? What am I trying to do? Who am I trying to impress? What is it for? We need to change the way architects think and create.

I haven't looked at magazines for the longest time. I'd rather look online at people's written work about justice and architecture, ethics in architecture, and so forth. So, why are we discussing magazines then?

SAF

That's a good question. I hope that conversations like ours will help shift the paradigm. You yourself have had a unique journey as an architect, and you've also produced a powerful manifesto that envisions a new era for architecture. This is apparent in the principles of "barefoot social architecture" and in your teaching.[4]

"Barefoot social architecture" is Lari's grassroots design philosophy, offering a women-centered and carbon-neutral approach to developing the built environment in Pakistan.

How do you hope to use pedagogy to advance the profession of architecture in the context of the global climate crisis?

YL

I hold all young people in great esteem. They are thinking about this and want to go in a different direction. I'm trying to connect to as many students as possible, to talk to whoever wants to talk to me.

I talk about the Global South in all my lectures and seminars. I don't have experience in any other part of the world. I've never had the desire to work anywhere else. All my work is in Pakistan, my own country, which I feel very passionate about. I know my people. That's why I want to work here, because I think if I do something, maybe I can make a difference.

I have an understanding of tradition and of my own culture, and I want to use it to improve the lives of others. The whole purpose of architecture, for me, is to bring women dignity. How can we make sure that through architecture, we provide women an elevated status in their own society, where people understand the value of their work? It's a different way of practicing architecture. Maybe it's nonarchitecture. What we call it doesn't matter to me. I think that if I have certain skills and knowledge, then I need to use it for the betterment of humanity. I am hopeful that we can change the way architects look at the world and look at their own role. If we don't, we'll become redundant.

SAF

I think it's important to recognize that these questions about justice and climate are very new to the pedagogy. There's so much information and knowledge that we can get from the rest of the world. In one of your talks, you said that you disagree with Bill Gates, who believes that rich countries are best equipped to develop innovative climate solutions. Your work has always emphasized the significance of the vernacular, of community involvement, of self-financing. In this talk, you highlighted the low-tech, low-impact solutions that are found in the Global South. These rich traditions of tangible and intangible heritage could help fashion an equitable world based on local wisdom and vernacular techniques. And you actually prove it with your work, especially regarding climate disasters in Pakistan. Could you talk more about the role of developing indigenous knowledge and wisdom to respond to the problems that climate change is causing? What would this mean for wealthy countries?

YL

While I was reading Gates's book, I felt that it had a superior attitude about what the West could do.[5] I guess when you have a lot

Bill Gates, *How to Avoid a Climate Disaster: The Solutions We Have and the Breakthroughs We Need* (New York: Knopf, 2021).

of money, you feel that you can do anything. But to me, money has never been important. I think when you don't have much money, you find creative ways of surviving, and you can do a lot with very few resources. That's what I think the Global South demonstrates, that people can have nothing yet know how to survive.

The whole Western world thinks that if they give charity to the poor like us, then that's all we'll need. But I would rather not accept any charity. I'd rather try to see what we can do ourselves and survive on that. We have seen a lot of money coming into my country, and the poor are still in the same position. More than half of the people are still below the poverty line. So, all this money that's coming in, for God's sake, what is it doing?

I've proven that for 40,000 rupees, you can not only rehabilitate a family but allow it to become self-sufficient.[6] In ten weeks,

Rs. 40,000 Pakistani rupees is equivalent to about $150 US dollars.

a thousand families who had nothing now have water, solar power, toilets, a one-room house, and the *chulah* that they've built.[7]

Developed by Lari in 2014, the *chulah* is a cookstove made from locally sourced mud and lime-plaster and fueled by agricultural waste instead of firewood. The *chulah*'s design reduces the risk of skin burns and respiratory and heart problems caused by cooking on an open fire.

Each household is engaging in what I call a barefoot enterprise, producing some kind of food product like fish, chickens, goats, or vegetables. Within ten weeks, they no longer want for anything because they're self-sufficient. That's my vision, and I believe we can do it.

SAF

These are the same conversations that you and others were having in Pakistan and other developing countries even before the 1980s. How might design replace these persistent Western aid models?

YL

I feel we didn't take the opportunity to really lift people out of apathy through design. Design is very important to me; it's what I was trained for, and it's what I value more than anything else. I believe that design is not only for the rich but also—and even more so—for the poor. That's one thing I want to put down quite clearly. I go directly to people. I try to preserve and conserve as much as I can. I use earth, bamboo, lime, and I use these materials in the best possible ways. It's the same log, the same bamboo structure, but there are a thousand ways of treating it.

If you're an architect, you have to make sure that design is paramount. That's what brings you pride, that's what brings your creativity, and so on and so forth. But when I design a *chulah*, it's never fully my design. What I have done is create a canvas to which everybody can contribute, and you can then see how it emerges as a beautiful piece of art. This is what I look for in my work, that somehow I am able to create opportunities for others to take pride in what they have.

SAF

What redirected your focus toward rural issues?

YL

I work in rural areas because disasters are impacting the people who live there more than anywhere else. Every time you have an earthquake or a flood, it's those people who are affected the most. You have to go there and find a solution. I believe that if we were to improve the quality of life in rural areas, there would not be as much pressure in the urban areas. I want really good designers to be in this whole disaster game. You need people with a lot of commitment, with heart, and with good design sense to be there.

fig. 5 Mimar 8

ARCHITECTURE
IN DEVELOPMENT

MIMAR 8 · 1983

I'm trying to see whether universities in Pakistan will join hands and go to rural areas. I want young people to be involved, because there's a lot of research and work to be done.

SAF

I did my undergrad in architecture at a university in Pakistan. I do believe even though the design education was good, we didn't really learn what was happening in our own country. Seven years ago, when I was in school, the only information I would get online was from sources like *ArchDaily* or *Dezeen*, talking about international work, Western work. My education was very lacking in indigenous and vernacular knowledge. Do you think we don't have a relationship with these ideas that you're talking about because it's not part of pedagogy?

YL

There are a couple of things that I'm trying to initiate whenever I talk to deans or schools of architecture. Firstly, I'd like to find a way to create an architectural incubator in universities where they can provide space and potentially corporate sector funding to young people who would like to go into nontraditional fields. Why can't architecture universities do this? It's not that they are short of money or that corporate sector funding wouldn't be available.

Secondly, there are many architecture practices that are doing extremely well. Why is it that they don't have a pro bono wing, like lawyers do, where the architecture practice pays employees to provide free services or minimum-cost services to under-served communities?

And third, we need to redefine the process of training for architects today. Every university is going along the same old ways. Nobody is interested in changing, because change is difficult. You have to work on it. But unless universities adjust, architects will become irrelevant. I think they are already becoming irrelevant, actually.

SAF

You say that the architect is irrelevant right now, so how can we redefine our roles? I think what you were describing is that the evolution of the designer or the architect could be the path you are on right now. That's a very interesting transition to observe.

YL

Why are so few of us participating in this? Why are young people not there with us? You tell me. In all these years I've never understood.

Today, there's a lot of money in disasters, worldwide. Many people come from abroad as consultants and tell us what we should be doing.

SAF

When you were commissioned to design the Taj Mahal Hotel in Karachi in 1981, there was an overarching assumption that expertise for these kinds of big projects didn't exist in Pakistan, and so jobs like this were usually given out to foreign consultants. I think the same conversation continues today regarding the expertise required to address climate issues. Why does this continue?

YL

We know our condition; we should be able to respond better than anyone. The thing is, you have to develop a certain expertise. It took me a long time to develop mine. I had never worked in the field, had never been to the mountainous areas, nothing. I had no idea where I was going. But you learn on the job. Now it's possible to learn without going through all that hardship, but one has to have interest. How does that interest come about? I don't know. That's why I started my lecture series, so I can get out and talk to people. I started the videos because I didn't know how else to do it. So that everybody has at least one safe room. That's all I want.

fig. 6 Mimar 11   *fig. 7 Mimar* 19

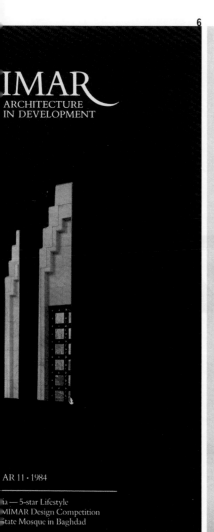

6

MIMAR
ARCHITECTURE
IN DEVELOPMENT

AR 11 · 1984

ia — 5-star Lifestyle
MIMAR Design Competition
State Mosque in Baghdad

7

MIMAR
ARCHITECTURE
IN DEVELOPMENT

MIMAR 19 · January — March 1986

Regionalism and Architectural Identity
Geoffrey Bawa of Sri Lanka
Beijing Guide

Mae-Ling Lokko & Benin Bronzes

Sumayyah Súnmádé Raji & Mae-ling Lokko

People assume you know so much about your history because you grew up in Africa, but this is untrue. We still ask questions about home and life before our time, and these artifacts are the only records left. The further away you are from home, the more questions you have.

MAE-LING LOKKO

I think many people, including myself, can identify with that. Often we leave home only to come back and look with more eager searching eyes to discover our own histories and define what knowledge is to us. So, I can totally relate to that.

SSR

Even in design school, the modes of storytelling that one grows up with don't carry over. I've often thought about how artifacts can amplify my design sensibilities by reconstructing memory, either spatially or culturally.

ML

I think it's a really important project for all of us, those from previously colonized contexts and those who live in contexts that did colonization. That work is on all of us. The museum and the university have been at the helm of collecting and organizing knowledge to support the colonial project. These are the places where this work needs to happen, both in public and intimate conversations like this.

SSR

How can we reclaim memory through this journey of return? In my journey to reclaim lost memory, I've often had to speculate because there are many gaps in our history. At times, the answers one seeks are to be found abroad, and it takes a certain degree of privilege to be able to access and interpret those archives. I wonder what this journey has been like for you. What has it taught you about your history, and how have you facilitated a return of memory, knowledge, culture, and storytelling?

ML

I've been very aware of how the power of fragments, which we find as part of our material culture, can activate lines of questioning and deepen our investigation into our knowledge systems. That hasn't necessarily happened through actual acts of making but rather by looking at our material heritage differently.

My dad used to tell me how when he washed his hands after a meal, his mom would put moringa leaves into the water for him to soak his hands in. He told me this while I was doing research for a textile company in Ghana that was trying to clean their wastewater using moringa. When he said that to me, I thought about how incredible it was that something in the leaf of the moringa plant is very good at attracting all this bad, heavy stuff and sinking it. There might be a way to leverage that insight, which people who worked with plants on a daily basis really understood.

A second, very quick answer to your question regards my research as part of Domestic Worldmaking by the Enslaved, a project that took another angle to understand the agency of the enslaved.[1] How do you cite different forms of oral tradition or

For Domestic Worldmaking by the Enslaved, a range of academics, researchers, and activists from around the world have developed methods to document the architectural legacy of the transatlantic slave trade. This project prioritizes the domestic architectures of the enslaved and formerly enslaved, architectures that were deeply nested within worldmaking and resistance practices, including agriculture, architecture, botany, textile, fashion, art, music, and oral traditions, and a broad material ecology.

archival material on a sort of canvas and allow them to sediment? This form of knowledge capture and redevelopment takes time and multiple voices; it is not fixed. Knowledge is incredibly subjective and context-dependent. Thus, while the project is years from completion, it has already informed my thinking around our material agency, our material heritage, and what that can reveal about our environment, our knowledge systems, and, ultimately, our own identities.

SSR

I really like that. What stories do you think we can see, read, or hear by looking at objects or materials around us?

ML

I don't think these stories are heard because of the objects themselves. Rather, the people who make objects and situate them in places like museums, and the people who are supposed to be passive recipients of these objects are all involved in crafting these stories. The story is very much an ongoing project.

Museum curators and scholars further improve our understanding of the systems that influence the structuring of these stories and their participants, especially the political systems. Museum audiences and citizens are also much more active in terms of questioning where these objects come from, how they are extracted, and what testimonies are included. The stories somehow emerge from this combination of contributors. Thus a whole spectrum of stories can be engaged. For instance, objects that bear marks of use and acquire value because of that use are imbued with a certain type of story around the everyday. As someone who works with materials that were once alive, I think about what these materials tell us about the environments and times in which they were generated. Rare, high-value objects that we find in museums are connected to stories about

BENIN BRONZES

power, the organization of society, its labor systems, and its material economies.

Depending on the objects, there are many stories we might project and accept from them. But I am encouraged by the fact that this narration is becoming a collaborative process involving multiple agendas. The best stories come out of this continuous interaction. That's what we've discovered in the Domestic World-making archive: people's ability to offer different fragments of stories or to question certain facts that have been maintained about these objects actually enriches the objects' stories in important ways.

SSR

What is your earliest memory of a museum? How has your perspective changed since then?

ML

My parents tell me we went to a ton of museums when I was younger, but for some reason I've blanked out on all memories of them except one: We were living in Malaysia and went to the country's old capital, Malacca. The city was full of vernacular kampung houses, stilt houses made out of wood and fiber material, with impeccable craftsmanship. The museum was the prince's royal residence, a sort of kampung house on steroids. The fact that it was a house where the objects were contextualized in a bedroom, a kitchen, or a veranda blew my mind. It's something that I still think about. All of the Malaccan monarchy's wealth was somehow captured in the built form. It felt like an encyclopedia in many ways, where I was experiencing history in real time.

SSR

Did the museum primarily have Malaccan objects or other materials on display?

ML

I honestly don't remember, but I do remember thinking about the materials the architecture was made out of. Those were definitely Malaccan, made by Malaccan craftsmen and women. I also remember the museum not being air-conditioned, but it wasn't hot, either. You walked up steps onto the veranda, which prepared you to enter the dark interior of the house. That changing gradient of light and heat was a very gentle ushering into the museum. That was probably what stood out to me more than the objects, which just faded into the background in that childhood experience.

SSR

Your description doesn't sound like the typical museums I've visited. When looking at the bronzes, which are looted artifacts, I'm reminded that they were not taken from a museum but rather from a palace in the Benin Kingdom. As we think about the journey of return, I often wonder what the site of return needs to be to receive objects like these.

ML

If we were to copy the kind of role, access, and social value of museums that we're familiar with in the West and paste them into places like Lagos and Accra, we would limit the cultural impact and educational prowess these spaces can have. While listening to Victor Ehikhamenor, one of my favorite Nigerian contemporary artists, talk about the Benin bronzes, I realized that he describes them as objects connected to ancestors. There's a significant spiritual component to them. These bronzes were documentations of events and personalities at the palace. They are a living library, an ancestral platform, which we don't witness in some museums today.

Recently, I've been fortunate to visit Kwame Akoto-Bamfo's Nkyinkyim Museum in Ghana.[2] It's an outdoor museum that

The Nkyinkyim Museum is dedicated to archiving African history and heritage. The museum is known for using *griots*—respected and learned storytellers—to unravel the history, symbolism, traditional African religious associations, and philosophy embodied in the sculptures archived there. The experience has been specifically designed to guide visitors toward healing and restorative justice.

collects shrines and artifacts that people from the diaspora engage with by viewing and making. Through this process they also are coming back to forge new links with West Africa, where they believe they have come from. There's a whole series of events, from the rituals of entering a sacred space to the carving of a head shrine, that shapes a lifelong spiritual connection between the shrine and any visitor to the museum. This offers a prototype for a much more expansive and culturally relevant role of these objects in context.

SSR

I think artists succeed in being provocative because they don't have to operate within the same systems and structures as architects. These artifacts were recategorized as art through their spatial displacement. What forgotten connections and images can we see when we look closely and read them like texts?

ML

I love the selection of these four artifacts because I immediately began to picture four people. You've got the young female attendant-in-waiting—she's probably still alive, in a sense—the recently passed Iyoba, or queen mother; her deceased husband; and finally, the son of the king, the ruling Oba, who made the idealized head of his father. These four people, two of whom are alive and two dead, are connected by the altarpiece and the Oba head. There's a generational link in these last two objects,

BENIN BRONZES

fig. 1 Plaque or belt ornament. Benin Kingdom, Nigeria. Bronze.

and this family and the people around them immediately come to mind.

At the same time, when I see such intricate objects, I cannot help but imagine the power structures that controlled these material practices and their division of labor. Guilds in pre-colonial Benin date back to the year 900 and are very much tied to the beginning of the centralized monarchy. There was a shift away from independent craft communities toward guilds, which suddenly came under the monopoly of this single ruler. That power system is so important here. Similarly, when we look at materials, certain ones, like the coral, epitomize the monopoly around trade with the Europeans, who were mining and importing coral from the Mediterranean Sea.

This brings me back to the first photograph you showed, where three British individuals pose with the looted artifacts in a burned down room. They look relatively composed and not too threatening. The objects are organized around the floor, making a convincing argument for this being some kind of structured, organized system. But we know it was actually chaotic looting. From the burning of the building to the way these materials are scattered on the floor one can imagine the damage that was done. It points to a history of violent extraction and the non-valuing of the significance of these objects in Benin society.

The way these objects have made their way around the world belies that catastrophic, disruptive nature and its accompanying lack of understanding. Thus, while it's one thing to have these objects returned, there's another project around associating these objects with each other in a way that builds an understanding of the society and its meanings.

SSR

Looking at the damage to the altarpiece and the red stains on the apron, I wondered what decay or its absence tells us about the object. It could either point to a frozen timeline or a story that is continually in flux. How can materials or material properties help reconcile these gaps in Black or African history?

ML

Decay is something I value a lot because the way an object decays reveals so much about the materials that were nurtured or used in an environment. When I look at that cotton band and the sutures that hold tight to the coral beads at the point where one might tug or apply force, I understand something about the care that was put into making this object.

We often fight material decay, particularly in museum contexts. And in our built environment we like to coat, freeze, and

fig. 2 Interior view of a damaged roofed courtyard inside the king's (Oba's) residence in Benin City, photographed in the aftermath of the British military attack on the city.　　*fig.* 3 Openwork apron formed of strings of coral beads attached to a cloth band. Benin Kingdom, Nigeria. Woven cotton and coral beads.　　*fig.* 4 Openwork apron detail.

2

3

4

fig. 5 Head of an Oba, Edo Culture. Benin Kingdom, Nigeria. Bronze copper alloy.   *fig*. 6 Altarpiece tableau: Queen Mother and attendants. Benin Kingdom, Nigeria. Bronze.

5

6

saturate our materials so they never age. Yet, if we allow materials to breathe, to discolor, we discover lots of in-between material behaviors. Like with your own body, how do you allow materials to age in ways that support some of the behaviors they've learned over their life cycle?

I wish to see this celebrated in museums in liberating ways that reveal to us practices of care. For me, one of the most inspiring ways of working as an artist has been the practice of distributed production by El Anatsui. Taking objects that have been used and touched over and over by the human hand, he joins them together like a surgeon suturing a wound and brings to them a collective strength. His hanging sculptures yield a very different tectonic that changes with place and produces sound, giving life to otherwise silent objects. Curators are free to manipulate these sculptures as they see fit, and through that freedom the weak sutures and lives of the objects are revealed. Museums can thus move away from a predilection for the pristine and isolated toward new notions of display and interaction that reveal prior contexts and environments. Looking back to the apron, I love seeing the cotton decaying like this as a result of exposure to some environment. How can we celebrate the craftsmanship employed and the aging of the material as part of our material heritage?

SSR

The energy that these objects radiate is also something I didn't expect. Seeing the Head of Oba, I was struck by how displaced from its purpose the object was. I also wondered whether it would ever truly find that purpose again. This reminded me of our shifting relation to craft. In the Benin Kingdom, crafts were employed for the display of wealth in a manner that is rarely recognized today. How do you interpret traditional craft practices on the African continent, and how can we conflate the past and present to realize a regenerative future?

ML

Valuing craftsmanship goes hand in hand with valuing material. We have to track parallel shifts in our value systems as we revive crafts because we have materials without ascribed meaning. For example, coral had no material meaning until it entered the Portuguese trade routes and then became this sort of rarefied symbol of aristocratic connection in the Benin Empire. These value systems are man-made, and thus they are constantly shifting. A lot of the erosion around material values has happened alongside the isolation of research experiments from contextual knowledge creation.

We don't necessarily live in an age where everything can be done by hand, and not everyone today has the luxury of affording goods that come from craftsmanship. I'm excited about how new technological tools and reverence for high-quality crafts-manship might come together in a new-age African material culture. In this new generation of African aesthetic identities, younger generations are also beginning to question where things come from and what community made them. That's very much needed. It's part of a shift from passive to active con-sumers in this material culture.

The types of institutional models that can support this sustain-ably over the long term don't quite exist. Vocational education in West Africa needs a lot of support and revaluing. The hierarchy we've embedded among our professions, with artisans some-where at the bottom, doesn't serve us well anymore. We need to be able to support and value this craftsmanship because it adds so much knowledge and expertise to our everyday life.

SSR

It's something that we learn by doing and talking and sharing with each other. What do you think this way of thinking can do for architecture?

ML

The architect in the African context at the moment is very much operating in the 20th-century Western paradigm. She or he sits between the owner elite, or the corporation, and the consumer, which helps drive these extraction cycles. There's very little wiggle room for architects in that paradigm to do anything other than the status quo. Materials come from a catalog, and no one will spend their time and expertise doing anything out of the ordinary.

This way of thinking opens up a new role for the architect who is willing to occupy other parts of this broader material economy. It is an opportunity to work with waste collectors, farmers, and traders, because they are now the producers and a lot of our mate-rial byproducts lie in their hands. It is also an opportunity to work with emerging enterprises in African cities that do everything from logistics to waste collection to food delivery. How might an architect working with actors in this landscape rethink how things are made, serviced, or maintained over time?

It forces you to engage with people from different classes and industries. And you learn that value isn't just accrued by handing off your design or product to someone who can manufacture it. Rather, you develop long-term relationships with people who use your objects for longer periods of time. I don't know a single architect who builds in Ghana who doesn't get called back for renovations. We build incrementally, we renovate incrementally, and our service model is very much a long-term one with our clients. Embracing some of these characteristics of how we make space and materials might open up an expansive role for architects.

Melanie Boehi & United Fruit Company Photographs

Raphaele Tayvah & Melanie Boehi

"A picture is worth a thousand words." When we apply this saying to the visual archives of the United Fruit Company, a collection of more than 10,000 photographs that are loosely organized into manila folders and photo albums, there seems to be an infinite amount of words to consider. Someone clearly thought through the order in which they were placing them. There are thematic elements that tell a specific story about the company's operations. But, at the same time, there is very little information about who took these photographs. Sometimes there is a note on the back of an image, but this is only true of a very small percentage of them. I presume that it would have been company employees, perhaps company photographers, who were sent to document procedures on the United Fruit Company plantations. Whoever it is, they seem to have an eye for composition.

MELANIE BOEHI

Yes, they are so full of detail. You could think of these as street photography, but also, they're quite artistically composed. You get to see things that aren't mentioned in writing and would be hard to verbally describe even if there were extensive notes or captions. The images tell the story in a more compelling way, as if their producers had to convince a boardroom or shareholders that are far away. But obviously now we interpret them in a way that's completely different to their initial intention. That's why photographic archives and sound archives are so important. They also capture things that we now find interesting that were once coincidences of documentation. If we think about how this collection ended up at the Harvard Business School, somebody at the company must have thought, "Okay, this is valuable, so we don't throw it out, but we also don't want to keep it." Now it gives us so much information about the environmental history of the United Fruit Company and encourages us to think about how the collection can now be mobilized as a tool to tell of the violent, exploitative history of this company.

RT

This picture of the dock in Havana is easily a 1,000-word description of this site and then some. There's so much unwritten history in it.

MB

I think in a way, yes, it is 1,000 words, but then also whose words, what words, how do you tell these stories? And now it's just sitting in a box tucked away in an archive. So, at the moment, it's not speaking at all. I mean, I was just reading this book by Anette Hoffman, *Listening to Colonial History*, in which she writes about colonial sound recordings that are in archives, describing them as "caged birds" because they are there, but as long as nobody is listening to them, they are not speaking.[1] All archival records,

Anette Hoffman, *Listening to Colonial History: Echoes of Coercive Knowledge Production in Historical Sound Recordings from Southern Africa* (Basel: Basler Afrika Bibliographien, 2023).

including these photographs, if they're just sitting there not speaking, are not those stories of 1,000 words.

RT

I would love to see a comparative picture of these sites now: which ones are still plantations, which ones are completely stripped because they were monocropped and had a new life after being a plantation, and which are just sitting there devoid of life because they were so poorly cared for during these times.

MB

And that's why such historical photography collections are so important for a range of disciplines. Historians will find it interesting, but so will people coming from a natural science background studying the environmental impact of plantations. I'm still thinking, it's so crazy that these images are just sitting there. Imagine if you took them out of the archive and displayed them in a white-cube setting. It would look interesting.

RT

That would be an amazing exhibit. When you look through archives systematically, you start to recognize styles and patterns, but if the photographs were simply wall-mounted or even set out on tables, I wonder what else would become clear through the lens of the non-researcher.

MB

With this kind of archival document, I'm interested in reconnecting the photograph, who took it, and the place it first appeared. Maybe it was used in some publications, maybe the publications are elsewhere. Why did this photograph end up in the archive when others probably did not? Where are other physical parts of the company's history today? These archival materials become isolated through processes, but they are all connected to other documents and to people.

RT

The way that archival materials create this global web and the way they're able to share these projects and ideas to such disparate contexts—who knows where the other prints of this photograph ended up? They probably are scattered across the globe. And what's the trajectory and afterlife of these images, even in a geographically dense area? Would this image be treated differently in an archive at the Harvard Medical School, versus at the busi-

fig. 1 United Fruit Company dock construction, Havana, Cuba.　　fig. 2 Woodland prepared for planting, Meja Farm, Preston, Cuba.

ness school, versus the GSD? We see this, and we talk about the photographs for their visual qualities and also what those visual qualities represent.

This also brings up, for me, the role of visual documentation in colonial projects. How does that relationship between documentation and the colonizer's vision of the space play into how we visually think about these contexts today? For example, if we look at this photo of the port project in Cuba, there is this interface between this highly industrialized commercial colonial enterprise and the people next to the gate.

MB

This is a great example. Here we see the people in the shadows. Maybe that was a conscious decision of the photographer, or maybe the photographer just focused on this view of the harbor and didn't really pay attention, and it's a coincidence that these people were there. Either way, it documents such an important contrast between the colonial activities on the land and human occupation.

RT

It's the classic colonial narrative of "there was nothing there until we came in and built these docks and this railroad and created this relationship between the land and the country and the people." No mention of what the land was like before colonization or people's relationships to it.

MB

It is the foundation myth of arriving by the sea. The United Fruit Company arrived in Central and South America in 1899 and then cleared and planted tracts of land, created extensive railroads, and built processing facilities. And then they planted bananas to have food for the workers. These became a commodity, and then suddenly no longer did the bananas serve the railway, but the railway served the bananas. So this infrastructure story is very central to the banana story. It's central to all colonial history.

The focus on infrastructure in this image and the earlier ones you saw is so emblematic of the telling of the colonial story as a story of development: "There was nothing, so we came and we built railroads, we built roads, we built ports, we developed business. We made the land productive." I don't think it was a coincidence that these images came first: they probably were regarded as more important than the image of the actual produce.

RT

Another image that speaks to this colonial saviorism narrative is this one with the caption "Woodland prepared for planting." The word choice here says so much. In describing the landscape as a woodland, they are presumably evoking the idea of a mid-Atlantic or New England woodland in North America. This is obviously very different from any type of vegetative growth you would see in this tropical context.

MB

It's that colonial naming of plants and of landscapes after something that looks vaguely familiar but might be completely different. It would also be interesting to know what it was before. Was it just a natural environment? Did people live there? Did people use the land? That's another colonial strategy, to declare a land uninhabited and unspoiled and then either in need of protection or of development. I mean look at this image. It must have been inhabited maybe by people, but definitely by animals. It was a whole ecological system that was destroyed to plant a cash crop like bananas or sugarcane.

RT

Then there are images like this, where we see maintenance. The tools they're using to spray the banana plants, and even where the figures are placed, are so well centered.

MB

It's very beautiful. And then at the same time, what they're spraying is probably very poisonous, which is one of the aspects of commercial banana farming that is so violent. So many people were poisoned, all the disabled children, the sterile men, workers whose skin was ruined because they were not given any protective equipment but had to spray these plants. And that's exactly what we are seeing here. The people are seen as tools; there's no concern for their health. They're just like another machine to apply the spray onto the plants. An image like this is interesting to examine with a focus on the history of work, because initially it was probably taken to document some kind of science and innovation. We look at it now and can immediately read it as documentation of labor conditions.

RT

Obviously these chemicals are keeping the bananas from being infested, presumably by insects, but what are they doing to the other flora and the ecosystem as a whole? What else are they killing? And how does this spraying impact the fruit of these banana plants? It also speaks to a hierarchical relationship between the workers depicted in the image and the people "studying" the situation from behind the camera lens and then broader human–plant relationships as well.

fig. 3 Bordeaux spraying, Bananera, Guatemala.

This is such an important component of what we see in this collection of images: the relationships between people and plants. The plants are often cultivated as monuments or resources, but they also have their own lives. They are witnesses, and they are historical actors. And some stories can be told in a certain way because these trees, or some of these trees, survived and thrived. But also, it depends on the regimes of care they need and they receive. In these "ruined spaces," it's interesting to go and look for these trees that have survived. You think like, "What have they witnessed? What are the stories that they were part of, the stories that they told?" Finally, the stories that you can tell with them, even just the types of species that are present, add layers to or undermine these official narratives.

RT

The species of banana in these photographs is extinct today. When bananas were first studied to make artificial flavoring, the then-dominant species, the Gros Michel, was used. However, in the first half of the 20th century, this cultivar was wiped out by a blight, which was no doubt due to the monocropping practices of corporations like the United Fruit Company. Interestingly, we can still taste the Gros Michel bananas today in banana-flavored candy.[2] These photographs show where this flavor

For more on the history of artificial banana flavoring, see Johanna Mayer, "Why Don't Banana Candies Taste Like Real Bananas?," *Science Friday*, September 27, 2017.

came from.

MB

It's almost like an archive of taste in the form of a candy.

RT

Exactly. The way these archives of plants are preserved in these chemical flavors is so potent. It's become an entry or access point to these species that have gone extinct because of how we grew and treated them. And then we have other parts of this collection, like the photos of irrigation intake and the physical infrastructure needed on these plantations to grow these plants. Just the scale of this infrastructure compared to the scale of these relatively short plants brings in a whole other dimension to the memory encoded here. This infrastructure is so intertwined with the plants we see in this collection. If we look, for example, at this image of the mill in Preston, the railroad and mill building are foregrounded. Then scattered throughout are these idealized palm trees. We start to see here the relationship between these exotic plants and this heavy industry where other plants were removed to create a more controlled environment.

I often think about Krista A. Thompson's book *An Eye for the Tropics*.[3] Immediately looking at these images, I thought they

Krista A. Thompson, *An Eye for the Tropics: Tourism, Photography, and Framing the Caribbean Picturesque* (Durham, N.C.: Duke University Press, 2006).

exemplify what she describes as "tropicalization," making the Caribbean look like the tropics through this touristic or colonial gaze. The tropics *are* palm trees: it's an exoticization of the landscape.

They presumably intentionally planted the grasses we can see here between the railroad tracks. That use of a plant vernacular that is not indigenous to a tropical context speaks to the use of landscaping as a mechanism of control by the colonizer.

It's similar to the use of lawns as a framing device in images of the management mansions. The lawn is created to be looked at, but also the lawn is a place from which one can look at the wild landscape surrounding it. It's a way of designing this island of civilization and, in this case, industry. In the relationship between the buildings and the plants, there is this idea of "plant blindness," so that somehow people are conditioned to not see most plants. The only way they are able to attract notice is by being monumentalized and turned into these visual icons, as we can see in the palm trees.

Because of the colors of the photographs, the plants also flatten together. We don't see them as icons but rather only as parts of the scenery because they're in black and white.

Because they are exotic species, they must be quite labor-intensive, which introduces a whole other way in which plants operate as agents of visual control.

This parallels the level of labor shown in the growing, harvesting, shipping, and commodification of the banana plants. Yet, they are so different: one, the banana, is a commodity; the other, the human labor, is a tool. They exist in such close proximity, and at the mercy of the colonial ideal as enacted by the United Fruit Company. All of this, of course, goes back to the idea of the tropical paradise as an ideal. These documentary images show that but also an underside of the idealized and the level of infrastructure needed to support that fantasy.

fig. 4 Mill, Preston, Cuba.   *fig.* 5 Farm 6 — Irrigation OH intake, Golfito, Costa Rica.
fig. 6 Manager's House, La Lima, Honduras.

Imagine the hours of labor it took for people to grow these bananas and maintain the manicured industrial environment. These photographs also show the vulnerability of the colonial project because it relies on so much infrastructure. I'm sure these things break down all the time; they have to be repaired and maintained, whether that's the plants that are affected by fungi or by bacteria or something like an irrigation system that has a small part break.

RT

Because of the climate, there is also so much maintenance, such a high degree of work that went into these houses and the golf course on the plantation, with their manicured lawns and fluffy palm trees.

MB

It's such a fabricated environment. The palm trees add the tropical effect, the lawn frames the whole scene, and the dog is kind of a marker of territory, protecting the house, its owner, and the company. And then in the background there is what looks like a lush environment that is probably also cultivated to look that way. It's such a classical colonial way of landscaping to create this island of civilization and set it apart from the wilderness and the jungle. Then the question is: what did people do on the lawn? How was it used? Was it an object to be looked at? Did people picnic on it? Did kids play? How did it function as a domestic space? Who was and was not allowed on the lawn? How was it gendered?

RT

This also brings up the individual identities of the laborers. How did they interact with the larger projects of plantation and industry? What is that relationship between the domestic sphere, pictured here, and the productive sphere that is presumably within walking distance? How does the design of this landscape mirror the colonial-metropolitan idea of what a civilized home space looks like?

MB

Also, the question of fencing. Was there a fence around this property? We don't see a fence here, but I'm sure it wasn't an area that everybody had access to. Other than visually, how was it set apart from its environment?

RT

It's a highly segregated space. The golf course is similarly so fascinating because it brings this idea of integrating leisure into the work sphere. Who is actively using this space? Is it just the managing family or families? Is this there so that when representatives of the company from the United States come to visit they have a dedicated and familiar recreation space? Or is there a way of reading this as a business space? And how does that leisurescape inform the idea of paradise and of an idealized environment versus a business environment?

MB

Was it only men? Were women allowed to play? I'd imagine it was only white management. But who of that white management? Maybe there were class distinctions as well. Maybe it was more for the people who just flew in.

RT

Returning to the maintenance regime required for this space, if it's only being used a few times a year when an executive comes to visit, how is it used, not used, and then cultivated in the times when it's not serving its primary function as a golf course?

MB

I wonder if this was a space designed as something the company could offer to managers from the US, an enticement to accept a job far from home. We can also imagine this space as one of leisure to control them. Presumably they did not want management to get too close to the local population, and a classic element of colonial architecture used by these companies was housing management in a kind of gated community. There was a clubhouse, there was a pool, there were sports facilities, and it was all to control people and to keep them segregated from workers and from the local population. This is where the control of people, and the control of plants, and the control of the landscape all come together. It's this emerging collage, something that has been interrupted, but then through this interruption, these places develop lives of their own.

RT

And it is geographically and socially so far beyond the imaginings of those trying to control it. Presumably these grounds would have been designed and built by a team from the US or Europe. Once that phase of construction is done, they are likely not directly involved in cultivating and managing it, and thus how it cultivated and managed the people. And then we must compare management's housing to worker housing. As we can see in these photographs, their housing appears to have been shoved against the barriers built to contain it. The physical landform holds this small-scale housing development in place and does not allow it to spill beyond its bounds.

fig. 7 Golf Club, La Lima, Honduras.   *fig.* 8 Laborers' Camps, Golfito, Costa Rica.

7

8

UNITED FRUIT COMPANY PHOTOGRAPHS

It's literally in the name, "the camp." It is described as a labor camp, so it is probably in some place where there were not enough local people who were keen to work on this plantation. So, with its need for migrant laborers, who came from elsewhere in the country or from even further away, the company had to house them. And the camp was built in a way so that laborers could be swayed, controlled. This is evident in the panoptic view from wherever this photograph was taken. You can see every house, you can see how people move between with this cleared area at the back. It is almost like if people try to run away, you can see them. Then the space is clear for people to hang up washing, so it is not supposed to be a pretty garden space. It is supposed to be functional, and the few trees seem to do poorly.

RT

The lack of plants in this context seems to be a means of control, of cultivation. It is very manicured, but in contrast to the manager's house and the golf course it is manicured for function instead of beauty.

MB

If we could zoom in or walk around the camp, do you think we would see traces of gardening? Because that's what people also did. They were probably fed up with what they were given to eat, so they started planting their own food or herbs or kept chickens, or perhaps even cared for ornamental plants. People always use plants to make spaces beautiful that are not supposed to be beautiful. Even the small trees, they are functional. They would have given people a bit of shade, and maybe they made this a space for socializing. To answer these questions, we would have to try to connect the image to other archival sources to know more about what this image contains.

Jeffrey Shaw & Mark Rothko's Harvard Murals

Rain Chan & Jeffrey Shaw

fig. 1 and fig. 2 Original installation of the murals at the Holyoke Center, Harvard University, January 1968. The murals' proximity to windows led to significant discoloration in subsequent decades.

RAIN CHAN

There are, in a sense, two parts to Mark Rothko's Harvard murals. First is the original installation from 1960, when Harvard commissioned Rothko to produce a series of murals for a room in the newly built Holyoke Center.[1] The artist approached the com-

Though technically these works are large-scale paintings on canvas, they are colloquially referred to as murals due to their site-specific nature. The Holyoke Center is the main administration building of Harvard University, designed by Josep Lluís Sert in 1960.

mission with incredible specificity, defining the murals' placement and their accompanying "entourages," like the amount of chairs in the room, how the tables would operate, and even the curtains to be installed.

JEFFREY SHAW

It's an extraordinary work, made all the more interesting by Rothko's attention to the whole environment. You see the beginnings of a sensibility, even in a painter, to want to create an immersive environment where all the components—the architecture, the physical relationship of the viewer to the art—are all considered as part of the experience.

In my own appreciation of the history of painting, I very often see painters gearing their work toward a strategic relationship between the viewer and the painting, all the while understanding that people don't always stand in the same position. In the history of Renaissance painting, for example, perspective establishes a relationship between the real space of the observer and the virtual space represented within the frame. These two spaces are in a delicate relationship, and the painters understood that they were articulating this relationship. In the Rothko room you have an even more emphatic articulation between the space of the viewer and the ethereal space of the painting itself. Many artists of that time were moving in that direction.

I am also reminded of certain phenomena like expanded cinema, which is a strategy for linking cinematic space with the real space of the viewer. Installation art is a similarly immersive experience, one which fully recognizes the agency of the viewer and tries to create a choreography of the viewer's relationship to the artwork. In a way, the viewers concurrently become the directors, the editors, the camerapeople, the actors, and the audience.

RC

In this sense the churches and palaces with fresco-filled walls were the progenitors of contemporary installation art practices.

The second aspect to consider is the restoration and democratization of these paintings. Following years of damage from intense light, Harvard deinstalled the murals in 1972, storing them away until they were exhibited again at the Harvard Art Museums in 2014. The act of bringing works hidden behind the walls of the institution back into the public is an important gesture. This was accompanied by a restoration process which projected compensatory light onto the canvases, allowing the murals to be shown in their original colors without physically interfering with the paintings themselves.

JS

This non-invasive restoration by beams of projected light is quite extraordinary. What interests me specifically are the technologies that enable such a process. We have a whole range of tools today to digitize, reenact, and renovate. I'm very committed to the idea that, given these new technical capabilities, we can make digital doubles that can be conserved on a level other than the work itself.

With the Rothko paintings, a large portion of the effort involved trying to resurrect the memory of what the paintings were originally. And while there were some records of their original state, these records are not definitive. The process involved a lot of searching, as if you were looking at an ancient Egyptian mural and trying to understand exactly what the original colors were through circumstantial clues.

RC

It's a kind of detective process.

JS

Yes. But these days, we can create digital doubles, which are extraordinarily accurate. Even paintings can be scanned to such fidelity as to record the three-dimensionality of the paint. You can digitally reproduce the brush strokes and the textures of a painting. And, of course, you can photograph these paintings at an extraordinarily high resolution.

These digitization projects freeze the painting in time. Even if a painting undergoes a certain amount of degeneration, there will be a file referencing its historic state that can aid future restorations.

Such was the case at the Mogao Caves, where extensive murals were digitized in order to better implement conservation strategies.[2] Interestingly, the digital file, the recording of the

Excavated into a mile of cliff face outside Dunhuang, China, this ancient Buddhist site on the Silk Road contains 492 decorated cave temples. Its 45,000 square meters of wall paintings and over 2,400 polychrome sculptures are the largest body of Buddhist art in China.

murals, was also recognized as having a heritage value on par with that of the complex itself. This value was amplified by the inevitable degeneration of these stone-wall paintings: all kinds of

fig. 3 Comparative view of Rothko's studies for the Harvard Murals   *fig.* 4 Digital scan of a study for the Harvard Murals, tempera on purple construction paper, digitally enhanced for color accuracy.

3

4

climactic and microbial forces living inside the cave environment made degeneration inevitable. So while there is nothing one can do to freeze that process of entropy, a digital double does allow us to maintain a memory of that work at a certain moment in time.

You also mentioned this notion of democratization. We can now build duplicates of works which are equivalent to the original in terms of experience. This can't be done with all paintings and all sculptures; and certainly Rothko would be one of the great challenges, because of the invisible luminosity produced by the way he handles paint. But for many works, you can create copies that are close to perfect. And these, of course, can then be distributed.

Digitalization can help avoid the most damaging aspects of the cultural tourism industry. Going back to the case of the Mogao paintings, visits to these caves contribute to their damage, to their entropy. This requires balancing the longevity of these cultural artifacts and how physically accessible they are to people.

RC

I have been thinking about the idea of an artwork's afterlife lately. When Rothko first installed the murals at Harvard, they existed in an almost pristine state produced by the intentionality with which they were displayed. When restored and re-exhibited, their context and meaning had changed, even though the work appeared similar to its original state.

In the essay "Dis-Embodied Re-Embodied Body," you describe a process by which an artwork becomes more embodied within an interface, eventually losing its physicality and becoming pure information.[3] What is your stance on this idea of an artwork's

Jeffrey Shaw, "The Dis-Embodied Re-Embodied Body," in *Jeffrey Shaw – A User's Manual: From Expanded Cinema to Virtual Reality* (Karlsruhe: ZKM Center for Art and Media, 1997), 155–160.

afterlife? Does reproducing and restoring a work change its content?

JS

Certain works offer themselves to reinterpretation, revision, or reworking. Others don't. Within the worlds of painting and sculpture, you will see painters return to certain themes, addressing them over and over. This produces many iterations of a certain obsession, or a certain focus. This is absolutely a viable strategy. You might even say that some writers just tell the same story over and over and over, with some variation.

In my work *The Golden Calf*, I made a new version of a previous work because I saw an opportunity to reinterpret the original idea using up-to-date technology.[4] Or rather, I wouldn't say up-

Shaw explains, "Let me describe that process quickly and simply. In the original work, the skin of a digital virtual golden calf is a mirrored surface. It reflects the real room in which the work is installed to produce this paradox of a virtual golden calf reflecting the real room around it. At that time, in the mid-1990s, I could only do this photographically. I took a spherical photograph of the installation room and mapped it onto the reflective skin of the virtual golden calf. Recently, there have been significant advances in video technologies: instead of just reflecting the room photographically, I can reflect the room videographically. In other words, I can have video cameras record the real environment of the exhibition room and texture that onto the skin as a real-time reflection. This was something which was technically not possible in the mid-1990s."

to-date, but I would say the work was originally made with the technologies of the mid-1990s, and the technologies that are available to me now are different. As a consequence of that difference, I can reformulate that work and give it a different look and feel. At its core it's the same work: it addresses the same topic and the same argument. But I'm now reframing that work; it's a kind of restaging. Suddenly there is a technical capability available which adds new aesthetic, conceptual, and experiential layers to the work.

RC

Two versions of a similar idea yield very different results for the viewer.

JS

That's one aspect of the topic. The other aspect that you touched on, which I think is interesting, relates to the question: what is the absolute nature of a work in time? When a work is created, it's created at a certain moment, in a certain cultural context and set of relations. Perhaps it's exhibited at a specific gallery at a specific moment under specific political conditions, social conditions, weather conditions, whatever.

That moment is irreproducible and, as such, the work belongs to it. Once the work is taken out of that moment, that period will never be replicated. So we need to understand that the life of art is always in a state of metamorphosis. The Van Gogh we are looking at today is not the Van Gogh that people saw at the time of its creation. Our perception, our eyes, our thinking, and our understanding are different, thereby conditioning our interpretation and appreciation of the work.

This does not bother me, because the power of great art is that it's able to live on in different times and assume different identities and meanings. As a consequence of this, some works don't live on. You look at them and realize they are lost in time. You can always appreciate them as artifacts that belong to a certain past, but if you don't undertake an almost academic effort to enter and understand the context of their creation, they won't have any relevance in the present.

Yet, there are other works that have the power to reinvent themselves or to maintain coherence under changing circumstances. Admittedly, this process is never guaranteed: we cannot know whether 100 or 200 years from now people will look at the paint-

MARK ROTHKO'S HARVARD MURALS

ings of Francis Bacon and find any meaning there. Yet, for the moment, those paintings maintain their power and energy because of what they are and because of who we are.

RC

The idea of newness is crucial to the context of your work, which often seems to push toward new technologies and new experiences. Thus, I want to bring the conversation to the "new" in new media art, the field in which you operate. Is newness—whether creating new experiences, new interfaces, or new technologies—integral to your work? Or are these just ways to help you deliver a message?

JS

Using media that was not traditionally associated with art making was a way in which you could forge a new direction. In *Finnegans Wake*, James Joyce invented a language to enable a strategy of writing that was new. That innovation in language released enormous potential in terms of what could be expressed and said. My fascination with new media and technology is that these are powerful resources for enabling me to make artworks, which, under other circumstances with other media, would never have taken that shape.

The history of art is the history of painters and sculptors innovating because these innovations enable people to see anew, to actually see something and for it to stand out from all the noise of the everyday. Because we see the sunrise every day, we don't see it anymore. So when the painter paints the sunrise, they refresh our vision of that phenomenon. They refresh our vision, refresh our perception, and refresh our sensitivity. This often means refreshing our sensitivity to things that can be very mundane.

Similarly, in these murals and in other works, Rothko is offering us an opportunity to look at color and look at paint and look at form in its most elemental way. At their most basic, the murals build on the legacy of Malevich's *Black Square*; they reduce things to kind of point zero. From there, you begin to see again and to appreciate and understand a level of spiritual depth that can be embodied in just these subtleties of form and color.

I think it was Paul Klee who said that for him to be a painter, he had to dispense with the whole history of painting in order to rediscover what it was from scratch. And in a similar way, to innovate in art is to offer the audience the opportunity to start from zero, to see a painting for the first time in their life, and to appreciate the miracle of that.

RC

What you've described reminds me of the question of authenticity:

specifically, how we might describe an artistic process as one guided by authenticity of the self. By contrast, the restoration of the Rothko murals has a stronger parallel to a problem-solving design process. Do you see the restoration as authentic? Is the restoration itself sincere?

JS

The authenticity of restorations is a complex issue. Restoration is a way to help us get closer to what artworks originally looked like. In that respect, it's a meaningful undertaking. Similarly, the process of cleaning artworks that have accumulated grime and dirt brings back an original sort of glory.

Yet, there's also a question of the extent to which we accept the fact that the entropy of an artwork is its truth. Some might say the Rothko murals have suffered as a consequence of sunlight. Others might accept their current state and question any effort to recapture their original truth. The noninvasive restoration through projection strikes a middle ground. I would further appreciate a situation where the murals' restoration was projected only intermittently so as to view both states of the work and appreciate their difference.

There are some interesting stories about restoration that are also quite tragic. For example, in the early 1980s, there was a wonderful painting by Barnett Newman, *Who's Afraid of Red, Yellow and Blue III*, in the Stedelijk Museum. It was a big canvas, and some guy, another artist who hated abstract art, came with a Stanley knife and slashed it. He really reduced the painting to tatters. The Stedelijk Museum decided they would send the damaged canvas to a restorer who sewed it back together and then repainted it. When the painting returned to the museum, people refused to accept it as the original. It was a disaster.

As a consequence of the controversy, this painting is never on exhibition. Certainly the restoration of the work in this case was invasive and meaningless. Perhaps it was even more destructive than the original damage. Maybe one would prefer to see the cut painting than to see it painted over, right?

RC

Your idea of presenting both restored and unrestored versions to the public is interesting. In fact, when the restored Rothkos were displayed, many people became interested in the novelty of the restoration process. At four o'clock every day, when the museum would turn off the restorative projectors, people would go specifically to the show to see the moment when the original appearance of the murals faded away to reveal their current state.

fig. 7 Archival examination of the mural panels in the Fogg Museum Courtyard, June 1987

I think the Rothko project, especially the restorative part, heavily leans toward the idea of the medium overtaking the message. The magic of the restored work is encapsulated in the project of doing the projection and getting it perfect. Mediums and interfaces are integral to a lot of your work, almost embodying the work in some cases. I'm reminded of Marshall McLuhan's quote, "The medium is the message," from 1964.[5] What is your thought

Marshall McLuhan, *Understanding Media: the Extensions of Man* (New York: McGraw-Hill, 1964).

on that in terms of yourself and Rothko?

JS

So, let's put it this way, have you ever looked at a painting by Van Gogh closely? Have you had the opportunity to actually experience a Van Gogh painting live?

RC

Yeah, well have I?

JS

What it means to enjoy a Van Gogh painting is to walk up close, really close, and see the whole painting just dissolve into brushstrokes, which are almost a chaos of paint. And then to start to step back and see the image emerge from this chaos of paint. To appreciate that somehow or other, this crude material has been transformed into images and experiences, which are so refined, impactful, and meaningful.

I am also becoming more familiar with Chinese calligraphy: you cannot disengage calligraphy from the pure visceral appreciation of the brush, the brush strokes, the ink. The enjoyment of the medium, the enjoyment of Van Gogh's paint, the enjoyment of calligrapher's brush and ink work extends to working with new media. On the one hand, there is an appreciation and pleasure in how these materials have certain properties that can be exploited in interesting and powerful ways. The simple virtuosity of what a graphics card can do in terms of imaging is something that in itself is fascinating. On the other hand, this is married to what the artist does with those materials. It's the convergence of the virtuosity of the media and the virtuosity of the artist's handling of the media that constitutes the work. And these two things come together.

I'm certainly not a sort of technofetishist. My appreciation of a media artwork is, first and foremost, an appreciation of the way an artist has given form to the media while appreciating the power of that media. A perfect example is cinema. Cinema is a technological infrastructure that is extraordinarily powerful. The virtuosity of the camera, of the lenses, of the post-production, all comes together and becomes meaningful when it's given form

163

by the directors or artists who are actually building a work using this new media. You can see how moviemakers enjoy their media, how they know how to get the most out of it. And often our pleasure is to see the way in which a filmmaker gets a camera to do something it didn't do before or gives us an angle or a shot we haven't seen before.

And these are all in a way things that are made possible by the capabilities of the media themselves. So yes, the media is the message.

MARK ROTHKO'S HARVARD MURALS

fig. 8 Archival examination of the mural panels in the Fogg Museum Courtyard, June 1987

165

Þóra Pétursdóttir & *Herbaria*

Adrea Piazza & Þóra Pétursdóttir

In *Herbaria*, Leandro Listorti, the Argentinian director and film archivist, brings together plants and film to explore themes of classification, preservation, and decay. Through this unlikely pairing, the film depicts the processes involved in archiving two disparate things and the inevitable degradation that follows. Did you find this pairing of plants and film productive?

ÞÓRA PÉTURSDÓTTIR

It made total sense to me, and I thought it was really unexpected. I was already a bit into the film when I realized this connection, but it immediately made sense. It was nice that it wasn't explained to me, but that it revealed itself, or gradually grew out of watching the film. And in that sense, it became much more thought-provoking than if it had been laid out in the beginning.

I think bringing together things that you wouldn't associate with each other and allowing them to speak to a topic that they might have in common reveals other aspects of that topic. That was elegantly done in this film.

AP

In fact, it's demonstrating the concept of *Pairs* as a publication!

ÞP

That's a good point. It really makes sense to me to build interviews around an object. I haven't done much of it myself, but others in contemporary archaeology have. The important thing is not that people know the artifact beforehand, but that it triggers some kind of thought or memory that the discussion can develop around.

AP

That is precisely our hope.

Speaking of artifacts, in the opening scenes of the film, a botanist plucks a plant specimen from the ground and places it in the fold of newspaper. I was struck by this moment in which a natural object is transformed into an artifact. You've written a bit about how the natural and material worlds meet—could you speak about this moment of encounter?

ÞP

I thought this opening scene was so strong, because it's so material. It captures the tactility of taking these plants and placing them into this mobile herbarium, which is also quite fascinating as an object. And relating to your previous question, I was completely fascinated by the reuse of newspapers and, as it seems, the completely unconscious pairing of a plant and a dated page in a newspaper. I just became obsessed with that. What page is it? What's the date? What are the articles talking about on that

page? And how does that newspaper become transformed in dialogue with this plant that is suddenly resting on it?

AP

Yes, they both transform when they are brought together at that moment.

ÞP

It's quite fascinating. But it's a good question, when does a thing become an artifact, or an ecofact, or whatever you want to call it?[1]

Ecofacts, or biofacts, are organic material remains found on archaeological sites that result from human activity. Ecofacts can include things like bones, seeds, and shells. Artifacts, by contrast, are remains of objects made by or used by humans. Both have archaeological significance, and together they construct a picture of how a society interacted with an environment.

Throughout the film we are introduced to many different ways of knowing nature and knowing these plants. The different ways of approaching it, the different ways of trying to document and capture it. Everything from observing it in the field, to collecting it, drawing it, smelling it, touching it, and sewing it onto a piece of paper. I think that was really well communicated in this film. To me, it was not just about a plant becoming an artifact, because it was becoming so much more. It was becoming a description. It was becoming a pencil drawing. It was being reproduced in so many ways. And I think it's really important for academics to try to approach an artifact through different media.

In the scene where they're drawing the specimen, I loved how he described that he wasn't trying to recreate an individual, but rather a kind of . . .

AP

. . . iconic specimen.

ÞP

Yes, an iconic specimen.

AP

I loved that, too. That drawing needs to represent all members of that species. We think of scientific illustration as an objective practice, but in fact, if you were to draw exactly what you see, it might not capture the entire category.

ÞP

Watching the film and watching how plants were being picked up, I thought, "How was that one plant selected? What criteria are being emphasized?" A great amount of weight is put on this one individual plant specimen to represent its species. The same, I guess, is done in archaeology, through typology and the chronological and material ordering of objects, where "good" examples are brought out and reproduced in one publication after the other and become iconic for a certain group of artifacts. They are not only representative of one group, but also of a clear cut distinction between this group and other groups. And yet, if you were to really dive into the material, those distinctions are so much more blurred, and fitting artifacts into categories is often

169

a very difficult task. They don't want to be loyal to a single category.

AP

Placing an object in a display case in a museum or institution further codifies these tenuous categorizations.

ÞP

Absolutely. And the whole architecture and organization of the museum directs people to follow a certain route that often starts at either end of a linear timescale. Visitors are rarely confronted with mixed up categories or mixed up times. Of course, this has never been the case for any human being at any point in time: we've always had to deal with all kinds of different pasts around us.

AP

A few times in *Herbaria*, Listorti collapses time and technology, muddying the distinction between archival footage and his own. This style of editing results in an understanding of time not as linear but as overlapping.

ÞP

I have, through my work, criticized the idea of linear time quite a bit and tried to argue for the significance of different understandings of time: folded times, times that are mixed up. That's not to say that the idea of linear time is wrong or that it should be abandoned.

The way archaeological material comes to us is ordered to some degree through stratigraphy and so on, but it's also tumbled and drifting, and it's often difficult to discriminate between times. They are compressed and physically touching. I become intrigued by this invitation from archaeological source material to think differently about time.

AP

There's something very fixed about the moment that we press a plant or the moment that we put a film on a shelf in an archive. It freezes time, in a way. How do you think about archives and time?

ÞP

The way I have thought about archives in my work is as living organisms. I think what was shining through in the film also is this idea of the archive not as a time capsule but as a living space, or a space for living things that continuously change and come into contact with unexpected objects, like the newspaper and the plants.

When I was doing my PhD, I was working with the herring industry in Iceland, specifically with two factories that operated until 1950 or so and then were more or less abandoned. In one of the buildings, I came across an archive in an attic that was completely covered in paperwork, which was tumbled around and soggy and completely unorganized. But the archive I came across in that attic spoke to me in a completely different, maybe more archaeological way. It triggered these ideas

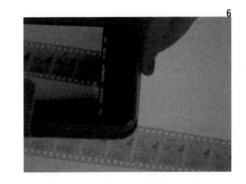

fig. 7 Herbaria, 01:01:52

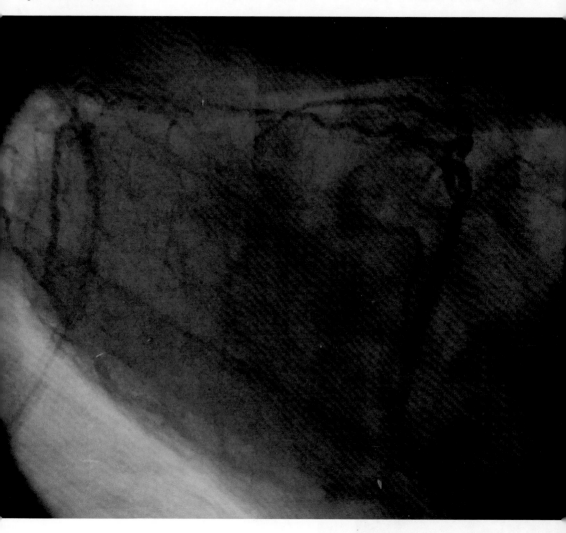

HERBARIA

of what an archive is, how things become archived, and whether nature can archive itself.

AP

I loved reading about that stockroom in your essay "Things out-of-hand: the aesthetics of abandonment."[2] What struck me most was this

Þóra Pétursdóttir, "Things out-of-hand: the aesthetics of abandonment," in *Ruin Memories: Materialities, Aesthetics and the Archaeology of the Recent Past*, eds. Bjørnar Olsen and Þóra Pétursdóttir (London: Routledge, 2014), 335-364.

idea of sensing things rather than *making sense* of them. I think nature can archive itself in a way that's removed from our own morals, biases, and ideas of how things should be organized and sorted. And in a way, extracting artifacts and re-sorting them in our way is exerting control over nature.

ÞP

Yeah, exactly.

AP

The film invokes the idea of the monster as a way to push against our desire to categorize or, perhaps, domesticate things.

ÞP

They talked about how the monster escapes that domestication. I think it could definitely be associated with drift matter. I also thought about Timothy Morton's notion of the hyperobject, which is this really vast object that is impossible to grasp at any moment, or in any place, or through any one approach or medium.[3] It's vast and minuscule at

In his 2013 book *Hyperobjects: Philosophy and Ecology after the End of the World*, Timothy Morton coined the term "hyperobject" to describe things so unfathomably vast that they evade spatiotemporal specificity.

the same time because it's everywhere and nowhere at the same time. Like climate change, or pollution, or drift matter.

I think it has so many parallels in the idea of the monster, in Frankenstein, in this phenomenon that transgresses our categories. The film explains the etymology of the concept of the monster and its relation to the warning.[4] This idea is also interesting when you think about it

"Monster" derives from the Latin *monere*, meaning "to warn."

in connection to those issues I mentioned. If you tune into it, you'll hear the warning.

AP

It's trying to tell us something.

ÞP

Yes, it's trying to tell us something. When we talk about warnings, we often talk about extinction, about losses, about things that are no more. But warnings can also be monstrous, for example, in the form of drift matter. The film focused on loss and degradation, but warnings are also building up around us in forms of matter drifting and accumulating in unforeseen places.

AP

The idea of loss is so present in archaeology. The notion that things are lost and buried underground, waiting to be found, is very one-sided. As soon as an object is found, it's lost again, in this instance to the ground.

ÞP

And objects are not really awaiting our arrival. In many cases, we cross paths only for a moment. They've been around for a long time before we encounter them. Our arrival is not necessarily a turning point in the life of an object.

AP

Perhaps more than other areas of study, archaeology is at once physical and philosophical, embodied and esoteric. It's one of those disciplines in which the extremes are very extreme. I think architecture is similar in that way. In reading essays about archaeology, I've come across many of the same theorists and ideas that are popular in architectural writing.

ÞP

It's interesting to hear you say that, because I often find inspiration in work that springs out of architecture. Maybe what connects them is the way these disciplines are based on physical things and bodies in physical space. I sense a lot of resonance there.

AP

Archaeology, like architecture, has an ingrained representational language. Orthographic drawings have long dominated architectural representation. Even as this visual language grows and begins to incorporate other types of representation, it maintains bias within it— in the hand of the architect, the Western pedagogies that undergird architectural education, the histories of these representational forms. How can we break the cycle of exclusion and open up expression to wider contexts, experiences, and backgrounds?

ÞP

Like so many other academic disciplines, archaeology has been centered around a very specific kind of writing. To me, it's extremely tempting— and I think fruitful—to try to break that paradigm and experiment with other forms of expression. As a discipline, archaeology has been very open to experimenting with new technology for documentation. And we archaeologists welcome it not entirely without question, but we don't problematize it in the same way as when we think about how we communicate knowledge to an audience. That's when we start questioning things more seriously, I think.

HERBARIA

fig. 8 Herbaria, 00:54:04

3D scans and photogrammetry, for example, have become ubiquitous in archaeological documentation.[5]

Photogrammetry uses data from photography to obtain spatial information about physical objects and environments at any scale. Archaeologists often use photogrammetry as a surveying tool to generate precise 3D models of complex features in great detail.

Oh yeah, absolutely. In the last five years or so photogrammetry has completely exploded. It's almost held on a pedestal as a way to record things in even more detail and more fully. But when it comes to the communication and dissemination of our work, that has for the most part remained a strict academic text following the rigid format of an academic article. I think it's very important, of course, to constantly evaluate our procedures at any stage.

I find it interesting that we are more conservative when it comes to communication than when it comes to our methods of documentation. We talk about outreach and the significance of reaching a broader public, but I think in order to do that we need to think through different media, different forms of dialogue.

"Drift" was the first essay of yours that I read, and I felt, as an outsider, that it welcomed me into the discipline in a really open way.[6] It feels

Þóra Pétursdóttir, "Drift," *Multispecies Archaeology*, ed. Suzanne E. Pilaar Birch (London: Routledge, 2018), 85-101.

outside of the strict disciplinary format.

What I love about your writing is that it really gives agency to the arti-fact or to the site. These things exist whether or not we're there to look at them. They have this life beyond us. There's something very hopeful about your work and its future orientation. It helps us expand the time-scale of things, and over time, this reorientation could help us under-stand that we have to treat differently these things we encounter for one day in our lives. Do you find your work hopeful?

Maybe I shouldn't be the judge of whether my work is hopeful or not, but it is definitely an aim of mine to approach this drift material in a constructive or hopeful way. Thinking of objects as disposable is not very hopeful. Being hopeful for the future of things is good, but it's also very daunting. When you approach things in that way, you also realize that they have autonomy, that they have a life beyond this momentary and sometimes incidental encounter with you and your actions. I think that's very important to realize, in order to be able to treat them in a more sensible way. So to me, it's not an entirely happy-go-lucky way of going about the world. It can be quite a serious way of realizing how things work.

HERBARIA

Herbaria carefully depicts the limitations of archiving and documenting things. In one of the closing scenes, it shows this old footage in black-and-white that appears on the screen and then dissolves. Text on the screen says that the footage no longer exists in physical form, because it was destroyed through the scanning process.

Archaeological excavation is often talked about as a destructive form of documentation. In many cases, the structure or the phenomenon documented will not exist in its original physical form after documentation.

AP

In order to preserve, you must destroy.

Stefanie Hessler & The Feejee Mermaid

CoCo Tin & Stefanie Hessler

For our discussion of the Feejee Mermaid, perhaps we can start with the mermaid's context—oceans—which requires us to re-orient ourselves and our thinking in wet environments. Where would you situate oceans as a concept or s/place?[1] For me, the

S/place is Trinidadian poet and writer M. NourbeSe Philip's term, which she uses in her essay, "Dis Place— The Space Between." As she states, "for the Black woman, place and space come together in the New World as never before or since. . .inner space is defined into passivity by and harnessed to the needs and functions of outer space—the place of oppression." S/place is used throughout this conversation to raise awareness about the systems that make space or locations unevenly safe and able to be claimed by cultural or personal identities as place. M. NourbeSe Phillip, "Dis Place—The Space Between" Blank: Essays & Interviews (Toronto: Book*hug, 2017), 254.

ocean so effortlessly disrupts this nature-culture binary.

STEFANIE HESSLER

The ocean disrupts numerous binaries—in the way that it floods, in the way that it is not containable by the fictitious borders we impose onto supposedly solid land and which even land evades (even though these borders are violently effective in practice). The oceans are very powerful, both as metaphor and as real mate-riality. To me, being in touch with water is crucial. There's this term "ocean users," coined by Leah Maree Gibbs, which means a user of that space or somebody who has experienced the ocean.[2]

Leah Maree Gibbs and Andrew T. Warren, "Transforming Shark Hazard Policy: Learning from Ocean-Users and Shark Encounter in Western Australia," Marine Policy, Vol. 58 (August 2015), 116–124.

This engagement allows for different ways of thinking about the ocean and speaking about it—or rather with it. Working with artists but also being in direct contact with the specificity of salt-water as a material is important to me, even if we need to ac-knowledge that not everyone can have this contact and that water has historically also formed parts of violent histories—not least during forced migration, past and present.

CT

I'm sensing specificity in your words. You've said "ocean" and "saltwater" but never "sea" or names for other bodies of water. I'm curious, can you tease out the difference between oceanic work, and say, work on seas?

SH

If we think of the planet from the perspective of water, oceans have a very different role in that they connect continents and land masses that are, perhaps, in a Western worldview, often seen as disconnected. Tongan and Fijian writer and anthropologist Epeli Hau'ofa teaches that land masses are connected by the ocean, not divided. The stickiness of saltwater is crucial, as it pushes against ideas of smoothness and notions of even flows that modernity's ideas of fluidity might suggest. Its salinity poses a kind of resistance, and the salt it contains is also part of our

bodies. The materiality of saltwater and the oceans as both a real
and metaphorical space has been the focus of a lot of my curatorial work and writing. Of course, rivers are connected to the sea
and to the ocean as well. I am interested in the connectedness
of these bodies of water and simultaneously in their specificities.
Melody Jue writes beautifully about the materiality of seawater specifically, or saltwater, and this is where my thinking goes
as well.[3]

These ideas are elaborated in Melody Jue's book, *Wild Blue Media: Thinking Through Seawater.*
(Durham: Duke University Press, 2020).

CT

I love Melody Jue's milieu-specific thinking, and I think it very
quickly points out a lot of gaps and cracks in the Western Enlightenment framework that is based on a very specific s/place,
environment, and time. Of the many seawater creatures, the mermaid is interesting to me because its combination of human and
animal (fish) exists in almost every cultural imaginary. But they
also evoke Gayatri Spivak's ideas about planetarity in the sense
that there are hierarchies that guide global imaginaries.[4] Disney's

Indian postcolonial theorist Gayatri Spivak uses the term "planetarity" to criticize globalization
as an "imposition of the same system of exchange everywhere," or an expansive flattening. See Gayatri
Chakravorty Spivak, *Death of a Discipline* (New York: Columbia University Press, 2003).

animation of Hans Christian Andersen's 1837 fairytale hijacked
mermaid representation and made them into young, feminine,
beautiful creatures of allure.

Since we're both in the United States currently, I want to talk
to you about the Feejee Mermaid from the Harvard Peabody
Museum of Anthropology—the version that is usually deemed
"the original." This creature has held public fascination since
it arrived in New York City in the 1850s. Have you heard of this
mermaid before?

SH

I have, yes, yes, but I've only seen images of constructed repli-
cations of it, never the three-dimensional objects.

CT

Indeed, there are many of them around the world. The "original"
in the Western world is attributed to Boston sea captain Samuel
Barrett Eades. He acquired the creature in the West Indies and
brought it to London. What we do know today is that Feejee Mermaids were originally made by Japanese craftsmen, then bought
and sold by the Dutch in Indonesia. During the Feejee Mermaid's
return to Great Britain, it was stopped at importation. Officers
and anatomists debated its status as a creature (a once-living
subject) or a thing (a fabricated object). Already then, its authen-

THE FEEJEE MERMAID

ticity as a novel species was debunked, yet it was later natural-ized through its legal status as a "ward in chancery."[5]

Samuel Barrett Eades sold his ship, *Pickering*, without authorization in order to purchase the mermaid. The ship's owner, Stephen Ellery, thus appealed to Lord Chancellor Eldon for a verdict. As a result of Eades's misconduct, he had to gain the chancellor's permission before removing or disposing of the mermaid. The court decision subjected the mermaid in question to the same legal title as young women who married without the consent of their parents, that of a "ward in chancery." Jan Bondeson, *The Feejee Mermaid and Other Essays in Natural and Unnatural History* (Ithaca, NY: Cornell University Press, 2014), 43-46.

So what we see here is actually a composite papier-mâché animal. At two-feet, ten-inches long, the mermaid has the torso of a full-grown female orangutan, the jaws and teeth of a large baboon, a scalp of an orangutan's hair, patchy facial skin, artifi-cial eyes, nails made of horn or quill, breast stuffing, and a fish tail of the salmon genus.

SH

There's something about the clunkiness—or stickiness—of the Feejee Mermaid today; it's no longer about the ruse or any dis-cussion of whether or not this is a real creature. To me the mer-maid evokes questions of how we may return to a certain time period and subject/object, revisit the enduring assumptions around them differently, and learn from them for various futures. The compound of the mermaid brings to the fore concepts of nature, a simultaneous alienation and fascination with it, and a view on nonhumans as chimeras, as embodiments of Otherness. The history of colonialism and trade, as well as gendered notions of subjecthood and its objectification, our relationship with non-humans, and scientific as well as legal frameworks, all collide within the history of the Feejee Mermaid.

CT

And if it were up to me, I too would much rather stay with the un-canny feelings and representations evoked by the Feejee Mermaid, turning the tides of mermaid Disneyfication.

SH

You mentioned Spivak's planetarity earlier, a concept I refer to frequently in my work as it considers the planet as a complex, unwieldy entity rather than as a unified globe. I also keep return-ing to her term "strategic essentialism," because every now and then, it is paramount to be able to temporarily designate some-thing in what might be considered a reductionist way, to be able to name a systemic injustice even if it means suspending our critiques of essentialism for a moment.

In the case of the mermaid, we might also want to consider its spectacle. A spectacle of nature, of nonhuman Othering—a spec-tacle I see as connected to the monsters and ogres that are remnants of Romanticism, the disappointment with European

fig. 1 Harvard's Feejee Mermaid, on display at the Peabody Museum of Archaeology and Ethnology.

1

THE FEEJEE MERMAID

Enlightenment, and the alienation of industrialization. The Feejee Mermaid also embodies colonialist projections of what might be found in far-flung places. An extension of promises of riches and simultaneous warnings of dangers that might be found there, which were commonly used to justify conquest. The mermaid really embodies—and its body performs—a lot of these anxieties.

CT

Exactly. In examining the Feejee Mermaid up close, its material properties also perform specificities of display. For example, the right side of the mermaid is much better preserved because the left side is always on display behind glass. The underside, with the most evident seam, is also marked with its catalogue number in red paint, a sign of ownership.

In a previous curatorial statement, you said that you are particularly interested in exhibitions and texts that perform rather than describe some sort of subject matter. Can you talk a bit more about this performance, and is there some sort of material linkage to that?

SH

My interest in the performative, rather than in representation in a descriptive manner, is how I came across the term "tidalectics," in the poet Kamau Brathwaite's writing. He uses a non-descriptive definition of a worldview shaped by the ocean rather than by the dialectics that he says define Western thought. Brathwaite performs tidalectics through his poetry, mirroring the sea's rhythm through skipped syllables and other linguistic patterns from his native Barbados. He has this beautiful quote, "The hurricane doesn't roar in pentameters," which is a sort of antidote to the rhythms of Western poetry. His writing is informed by the Caribbean-Creole experience, by the oceans and hurricanes, by climate change, and also, of course, by diaspora and by the history of European colonialism in Barbados, which indeed came to the Caribbean via the ocean.

To me, the way he develops tidalectics through writing and poetry itself is really exemplary of the way that I think exhibitions can address oceans too, which is not to describe them necessarily, not to represent them necessarily, but to approach their subject matter in a performative way where this divide between the thing itself and its representation becomes undone.

Of course, we know from feminism and postcolonialism about the criticism and the problems and the violences that come with representation. So then my question for the ocean, or for exhibitions dealing with the ocean, is: how can we not only speak about but *through* and *with* and maybe *nearby* the subject matter?

In this sense, I am thinking, for example, of Vietnamese filmmaker Trinh T. Minh-ha, who has developed a similar methodology in her filmic work.

CT

I want to dwell on your feminist stance on performance because the Feejee Mermaid, in its history from London to New York to Boston, has always been spoken for, such as by Captain Eades in Britain or the American showman P.T. Barnum, who purchased it in the US; white men have always steered its narrative. What you see here is an advertisement of Captain Eades's mermaid by George Cruikshank, the same famous male illustrator of all of Charles Dickens's books. It was also in gentleman magazines and scientific journals, most often behind glass and fetishized.

SH

In terms of this particular object, and even mermaids in general, there's something particularly objectifying about them. Mermaids bring together non-human elements; they are hybrids created by humans. The use of these nonhuman bodies in a grotesque way is violent to the very beings of these animals. And there is also a violent gesture at play in the way that they are built to create the impression of a human—a woman, even if a fictitious half-fish woman. Also, there is the exoticism of a creature coming from the South Pacific. The mermaids were hoaxes, of course, but nonetheless attracted scientific and general curiosity in the sense of a *Wunderkammer*.

One might say that combining these animals to appear half-human is an attempt to pass them as both civilized and transmogrified. The mermaid also brings to the fore the age-old dream of being able to swim or live underwater or up in the air, certifying our natural state or the state that our bodies are in.

The Feejee Mermaid also raises certain questions: Whose stories are told? Who tells them? How? Zoological museum collections, as with zoos and aquariums too, offer displays for pleasure, curiosity, wonder, astonishment, but they are also places of exotification and control, places that promise to bring order to and mastery over the unwieldy realm of nature, including to those considered too close to nature—women and non-Western cultures.

CT

Most definitely. How and where the Feejee Mermaid has been strategically represented throughout history, and for whose purpose, is an inquiry inseparable from its materiality. At the Peabody Museum, it remains encased in a glass vitrine, which I think is much more akin to the logic of an aquarium, promoting dry and distanced engagement. Your curatorial work uses ideas of oceanic performance rather than the preciousness of encased displays. It is much more responsive to its contents. I love that it immediately bypasses a lot of the clichés of doing oceanic work or of oceanic representation. If you had to name how you curate oceanic work, which definitely does not adhere to aquarium logic, is there a term that you would propose for this?

SH

That's a great question. I might even go with the term "tidalectics," because it's a wordplay on the dialectics of Western Enlightenment, post-Enlightenment thinking, and on the tides, which are always in motion and changing and which are—like our bodies—responsive to the moon. So, there's an interconnectedness to that which I really appreciate and which I think affords us the ability to approach oceanic exhibitions and curatorial practice beyond ocean-centered exhibitions in a very specific way.[6]

Stefanie Hessler, "Tidalectic Curating," in "Curating the Sea," ed. Pandora Syperek and Sarah Wade, special issue, *Journal of Curatorial Studies* 9 (October 2020): 248–270.

CT

I'm thinking about your work as editor of *Tidalectics* and author of *Prospecting Oceans* (both published by MIT Press). What drew you to oceans or oceanic work?

SH

I find thinking with the ocean really generative, and I feel at home in water. Of course, it's important to acknowledge that not everybody is able to experience water or to feel an oceanic sense of pleasure. Editing *Tidalectics* and then authoring *Prospecting Ocean* were ways for me to dive deeper into this field, inviting other thinkers and artists into the conversation as well by commissioning texts that approach the ocean from various perspectives. This allows us to imagine, as Brathwaite suggested, how our worldviews might be different coming from the oceans rather than from land. *Tidalectics*, the exhibition and book, are poetic but also political through their poetics. *Prospecting Ocean* emerged from a cultural theory perspective through the lens of artists' work, with the aim to think about extraction in a more explicitly political mode.

The ocean asks for ways to approach our current moment of the Anthropocene from a different perspective, one that is not so much based in linearity, progress, and so on, but in really thinking about cyclical movement, repetition, change, fluidity, uncertainty. In this sense, tidalectics is an apt metaphor and methodology to grapple with the crises we're experiencing at this moment that are seeping more and more into geographies beyond the Global South, where they were already palpable and felt for a long time.

CT

It's so great to hear you say all of this because this is the sentiment I've been trying to tease out in the architectural world: to refocus our attention on oceans as more than the extremes of unknown-versus-productive and instead emphasize the decentering power of oceanic work. And as you talk about oceans in our so-called Anthropocene, I am reminded of Sylvia Wynter's citation about globalization starting with Christopher Columbus's Atlantic Ocean crossing of 1492 to the "New World." Do you consider yourself an ocean scholar?

SH

I come to the ocean from the perspective of a curator working with contemporary artists and thinking together with them, supporting their work, as well as inviting in thinkers and doers from other fields—oceanography, gender studies, Indigenous scholarship, science and technology studies, and more—and commissioning scholarship from writers to further deepen this inter- and transdisciplinary work. This expanded notion of a curatorial space has been really central to my thinking when it comes to the ocean as well.

As someone who works a lot on questions of ecology and its various social intersections, I feel that I need to be in contact with nature's materialities, with what Donna Haraway calls "nature-cultures." I want to speak about these issues not from a distance, which might reinforce the modernist position of humans as outside or somehow above the planet observing it from a bird's eye view. Since I work so deeply on embodiment and different ways of knowing, it is important to also acknowledge that a lot of what we talk about in reference to new materialism and new feminism today is rooted in ancestral knowledges.

CT

On the subjects of narrative, materiality, and display, I want to amplify the Japanese legend and site that has been lost in the Feejee Mermaid's long colonial journey from the West Indies through Cape Town to London and eventually New York and Boston. We do know that it was created in Japan more than 1,400 years ago. As the legend goes, a fisherman was caught trespassing on protected waters to fish, and, as punishment, was turned into a hideous beast by the gods.

SH

Interesting.

THE FEEJEE MERMAID

fig. 2 Two Feejee Mermaids at Harvard's Peabody Museum of Archaeology and Ethnology.   *fig.* 3 Hand-colored etching of a Feejee Mermaid in a glass case made by the printmaker George Cruikshank in 1822.   *fig.* 4 Illustration of reporters and editors examining P.T. Barnum's Feejee Mermaid, from Barnum's autobiography, *The Life of P.T. Barnum*, published in 1855.

And with his last breath, before this merman—if we had to specify gender—was petrified, he asked the prince to build a temple to display his mummified remains as an object lesson for the sanctity of all life. In Japanese, the term for mermaid is *ningyo*, closer to "human-fish," and the remains are still cared for by the Shinto order at Fujinomiya, in the Tenshou-Kyousha shrine near Mount Fuji.

It's fascinating that the Feejee Mermaid has a completely different origin story and place of origin than its site of display. In a way, this object has proliferated into its own genre. It has been adopted by other cultures and repurposed for different meanings.

The story is also not so pure. There's some literature that states that these Feejee Mermaids were quite popular in 19th century Japan, and Japanese craftsmen created a lot of them specifically to sell to and perhaps trick foreign buyers. So, there's a sort of rebellion in this dual exchange. It was not the unilateral hierarchy that we are perhaps used to in some of these colonial stories.

It shows that agency is not just a monolithic term or something that is only granted to one particular individual or group. Even in a bilateral exchange, different forms of subversion or methods of claiming agency have been and are practiced. It is not possible to reduce such complexity to a sort of dialectic or binary. This is where water or the ocean floods supposed certainties and simplified dualisms.

For me, the Feejee Mermaid as an object, despite its fetishization and its lost narrative in translation, tangles maritime history, environmental history, and also, perhaps craft and design history. They are material objects that can help move us toward more-than-human ways of being or the term "decolonial ecologies" put forth by Martinican environmental engineer and writer Malcom Ferdinand.

Are there any other objects that evoke the same for you? Maybe the Feejee Mermaid has been too overshadowed by P.T. Barnum and cannot actually point to these renewed aims.

I think that objects can—carefully—be transported into a different context or looked at anew. And that's what's also so powerful about the question of decolonial ecology. Malcom Ferdinand uses the poignant term "altercide," which he defines as the oppressive denial of living in the presence of an Other. Like ecocide, altericide is another term to critically look at the history of colonialism and imperialism and racism with an ecological lens.

Ferdinand's work offers a review or reconsideration of ideas centered around ecology from a decolonial perspective rooted in the Caribbean. And with objects like the Feejee Mermaid, there may also be ways of looking at it differently, as we have been discussing.

Though I still feel it objectifies nonhumans. We can look at objects anew but the mermaid cannot shed the history through which it first came to London and then to New York and Boston. A lot of the problems that we are experiencing today pertaining to the ecological crisis and social crisis we find ourselves in are based precisely on this approach of ownership or objectification of nature. So I think that the Feejee Mermaid is also symbolic of an object that is created for a specific purpose by humans.

CT

The provenance is also related to this objectification. The object is safeguarded and exhibited in rotation with its many duplicates to sustain specific narratives. There are actually two Feejee Mermaids at the Peabody Museum. To this day, we don't know if either one of them is the "real" Feejee Mermaid from Captain Eades or Barnum. Authenticity and realism are completely muddled in these fetishized objects. While we know about its complex history in terms of object authenticity, its current context stops short of proposing alternatives, preserving some of the structures that gave the object fame in the first place.

Architecture has been predominantly concerned with how to design for humans, and only in recent years has the discourse shifted to also ask, "Are we purely human (subject) or part thing (object) in our increasingly designed age?" We already spoke about the land/sea or wet/dry divide that's so persistent and how it's important in our age of climate change and the need for oceanic world views. I'm also intrigued by the larger relationships between zoology and anthropology (especially in submerged s/places) and how design objects reveal glimpses of this increasingly muddy boundary.

SH

The mermaids were often described as repulsive, ugly, or having died in agony. The question of zoology and other forms of display, at that moment of human zoos and other terrible practices of colonialism and patriarchy, are very much present in these objects that turn women and animals into exotic beings. So indeed, I think the Feejee Mermaid can be a starting point because it does represent and embody so many of these things that we're discussing.

CT

I'm from Hong Kong, and the Lo Ting fish (which more people are now aware of because of Cantonese-Swedish artist Lap-See Lam's exhibition, which you curated as director of the Swiss Institute) is a very specific marginalized animal state that's neither human nor fish.[7] You're German-born, you've lived in Norway

Lap-See Lam's exhibition, *Tales of the Altersea*, was on view from May 10 to August 27, 2023, at the Swiss Institute in New York City. As described by Stefanie Hessler in this interview, "the Lo Ting definitely is very present in Lap-See Lam's exhibition and in the way that she traces the origin mythology of Hong Kong, Cantonese language, the Chinese tradition of shadow play, and so on in her work, and in this case, for a sunken ship restaurant."

and now New York. Is there a mermaid from one of these cultures that perhaps you've heard of or identify with?

SH

That's a great question. The maps by Swedish cartographer Olaus Magnus actually had all sorts of sea creatures on them, including mermaids. Those creatures were really issued as both a lure and a warning for seafarers about all of the places and fantastical beings that one might encounter across the seas, but they were also a warning of what might happen if one fares too far from land or from one's own origin.

CT

So, somewhat similar to the Japanese legend.

SH

Yeah. And in Brazil, of course, there are the mythologies of the gender-fluid Mami Wata, which came from West African cosmologies and religions through the process of colonization. The mermaid is an interesting creature in that sense because it defies the Western binary of human and non-human, which is also present in the binary of land and water.

CT

We've ended on an interesting slippage between object and subject that mermaids and oceanic work afford. In wet environments, this binary is simultaneously magnified but also dismantled completely. Humans at sea need incredible machinery and equipment, almost to the point where we become objects and no longer subjects, magnifying the politics of who even gets counted as a being at sea.

SH

I love that messiness because I think that that's really where we're at. Everything is messy, and acknowledging that and then saying, "Where do we go from this point of messiness?" is what can lead to productive conversations and approaches.

THE FEEJEE MERMAID

And acknowledging that being in this messiness, and still being able to act from within it, is also a position of privilege.

In terms of the oceanic, not the sublime or majestic that reiterates or reinforces a sort of dichotomy between subject and object, I think a constant shift in perspective is actually what the ocean affords us. We don't ever arrive at one point of saying, "This is the object, this is the subject," or, "This is the thing and the creature," but there's flux and fluidity and things can continuously be approached through a different lens.

Oceans as a s/place, to think with and from, forfeits essentialism in a way where it momentarily allows us to stop; you can almost take a screenshot, like high tide and low tide. We are not at the static moment of final definition but rather in flux, revisiting and returning over and over again to the same question from different points of view.

Sergio Lopez-Pineiro & Williamina Fleming's Astronomical Photographs

Andrea Sandell & Sergio Lopez-Pineiro

ANDREA SANDELL

When I first pitched this conversation, you said, "Great, we're going to be talking about nothingness!" Were you just being facetious, or was there something that you were trying to point at with that word?

SERGIO LOPEZ-PINEIRO

The image you sent really looked, to the naked eye, like nothing: a sheet of paper that has been stained or that has gotten old and has accumulated specks from dust or mold, or something like that.

I'm looking at the images right now. They're very beautiful, don't get me wrong, but at first sight, they look like nothing.

AS

I am fascinated by how they might look like nothing—like old sheets of paper that have accumulated dust and specks—yet they functioned as exercises in measurement.

These photographs were produced around the end of the 19th century, at a moment when cameras were first being integrated with telescopy. This use of photography allowed measurements to be incorporated more precisely into astronomy and astrophysics. For the first time, the observation of celestial bodies shifted from a qualitative to a quantitative practice, specifically by looking at frozen moments in the night sky and registering differences across those frames.

An image like this might look like specks of dust on paper, but behind it lies strict quantifications of the night sky through graphs and very careful observation. This labor was carried out by a group of women who processed the marks on the photographs.[1]

Known as the Harvard Computers, these women astronomers worked for the Harvard College Observatory (HCO) between 1877 and 1919. Though they were hired primarily as calculators of astronomical data and received wages that were significantly lower than those of their male counterparts, their insights looked beyond strict calculation and led to significant contributions in the field of astronomy, many of which they published in research articles.

Many of their intuitions would prove to be groundbreaking in the field of astrophysics. These images that might appear as gestural hide within them a process that's incredibly measured.

SLP

The story is really interesting. The images that graph the change in intensity of light look like the precedents for what has become a very common spectral analysis of celestial bodies, as far as I know.

I think that this points to the beginning of the breaking down of something that is purely visual, like light, into something that is abstractly measured. The star is no longer a speck, the star is now a graph. It would be interesting to put these images in conver-

fig. 1 Spectra of stars in Carina. Photographs of globular clusters. Novae photographs and distribution graphs.

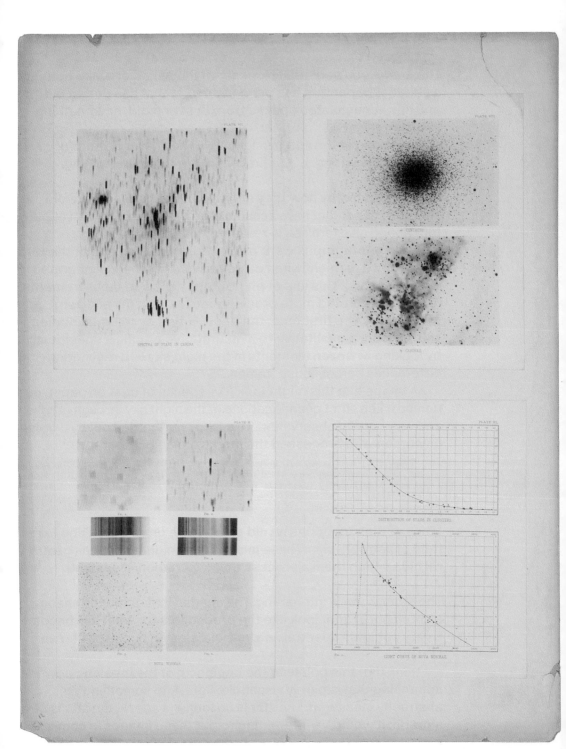

WILLIAMINA FLEMING'S ASTRONOMICAL PHOTOGRAPHS

sation with artworks produced at a similar time. Where do they sit relative to Impressionist painters' attempts to capture light as it perpetually changed? They also remind me of Man Ray's dust studies, insofar as some of these photographs are particularly abstract.[2] I think that at that moment in time, they were trying to

Man Ray's 1920 photograph *Dust Breeding (Duchamp's Large Glass with Dust Motes)* documents Marcel Duchamp's *The Large Glass* after it had collected a year's worth of dust.

figure out this tension between what they saw and how it could be represented and the means to do it. This tension emerged at a similar time in both scientific and artistic domains.

AS

In a way, the collection represents an inventory or a gathering of different conditions. And those that took part in this inventorying primarily used their intuition to explain the differences between the images that emerged. I know that you use inventories as well. Do you see these images as a type of inventory? How do you view the function of inventories?

SLP

I have used inventories as a design technique to discern one's own aesthetic preference, allowing that to become the sensibility with which to approach a project. Benedetto Croce, a leading figure in 20th-century Western aesthetics, wrote that intuition is an objectified impression, a particular image, not necessarily visual of course, that is held in a person's consciousness.[3] As de-

As Croce writes, "Knowledge has two forms: it is either intuitive knowledge or logical knowledge; knowledge obtained through the imagination or knowledge obtained through the intellect; knowledge of the individual or knowledge of the universal; of individual things or of the relations between them: it is, in fact, productive either of images or of concepts." Benedetto Croce, *Aesthetic as Science of Expression and General Linguistics,* trans. Douglas Ainslie (New York: Noonday Press, 1920), 1.

signers, we have a tendency to quickly construct images in our mind in response to whatever situation, to whatever commission, to whatever project, to whatever competition we have. It's an almost knee-jerk reaction. Our imagination is very active, and it's constantly producing these images, some of which we are able to describe, some of which are very ephemeral, continuously vanishing away while we try to chase them.

The inventory is a technique for working systematically with this intuition. It begins as a collection of images that little by little can define the rough, fuzzy boundaries of that objectified impression. At the beginning, it's a trial and error process, but there's a moment when any new image that comes in makes it so that other images need to leave. It's not just an infinite collection. You actually systematically shape that group, that inventory, to create what you can only sense intuitively, becoming as precise as possible. There's a moment when you start to be able

fig. 2 Photographs taken by the Bruce Telescope of the Milky Way in Sagittarius, the Southern Cross, the Vicinity of eta Carinae, and the Magellanic Clouds.　　　*fig.* 3 Method of determining Aberrations, Nutation, and Precession Constants. Photograph showing Eclipse of Jupiter's Satellite I, December 10, 1892. Method of photographing Star Transits 1888. Method of determining Stellar Parallax. Nebula in Andromeda showing that Parallax is less than half a second.

2

3

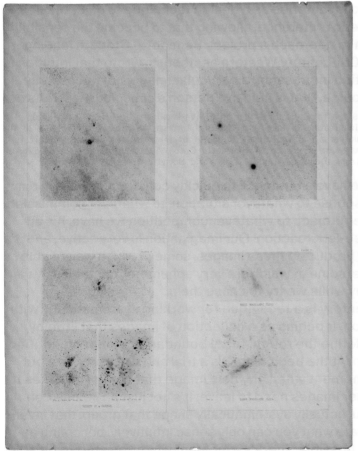

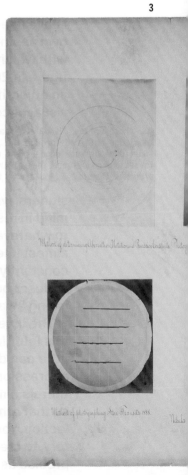

WILLIAMINA FLEMING'S ASTRONOMICAL PHOTOGRAPHS

to verbalize why an image belongs or why it doesn't. One can create an inventory without really projecting an image, without projecting a space, without projecting form. Rather, it's a process for systematically shaping our own introspection.

AS

It's not a coincidence that the words "inventory" and "inventing" share the same root.[4] Through inventories, you're not building

Both words find their root in the Latin verb *invenire*, meaning "to come upon" or "to discover."

the project, you're not being propositional, rather you're building the frame around which you can identify what belongs and what doesn't. You're beginning to build your edges. The middle is still vague, but perhaps the act of building the edges is the most important step you take, because it allows the middle to take form. When I first saw these photographs, I saw them as drawings as opposed to images. It seems as if drawings and images might play two different roles within the process you just described.

SLP

Images tend to be better at conveying atmospheric qualities. When dealing with intuition, it really helps when images are atmospheric. It's not a general position that I have regarding the relationship between images and drawings. It's about the particular circumstances of the process I've described. Drawings are often immediately concrete. They become real very quickly and transform our intuition—something that could be very broad and rich—into something concrete in a quick, dry manner.

It is true, these images look like drawings. Is that good or bad?

AS

Well, for me, the goal would be to develop a drawing that's atmospheric. At least that's the ambition I would set for myself. Perhaps these images are getting towards that, in a way.

SLP

What do you think about the fact that they're black-and-white?

AS

Apart from the fact that it's just a necessity of the time for photographs to be in black-and-white?

SLP

Of course, of course. Do you think that what they saw with their eyes—like slightly different hues in the color of the light—were not registered in the photographs they were analyzing?

AS

I'm not sure. What first struck me was that the way we usually see the night sky is inverted here: stars become black dots on a white background. That simple inversion of light made these look more like drawings than photographs to me. There are also

197

many effects—such as the pulsation or coloration of light—which at first glance these images don't seem to register. The photographs reduce or simplify their subject. Perhaps that's what made them so successful in allowing them to function as analytical tools for discovery.

SLP

The inversion of white stars as black dots on the paper is a very interesting one. It creates an abstraction where you're no longer sure what you're looking at on the paper. That distance allows us to look at the night sky a little bit more coldly or a little bit differently.

I think we don't pay enough attention to the emotional temperament we find ourselves in when dealing with the limitations of representation. A large part of the learning curve for any designer involves managing their own emotional distress due to their inability to register what they want to register, while also developing their awesome power to register things that they thought they couldn't register. Learning how to manage both the excitement and the frustration is integral to questions of representation.

AS

It's a topic that doesn't get brought up a lot actually. Something really great happens when you allow your emotional state to infiltrate your work. It spurs creative ways of representing things, so I really appreciate you bringing up this topic. As you pointed out, you can imagine the frustration when those qualities of variety and intrigue that you observe with your naked eye get flattened and abstracted on a piece of paper. Conversely, when you allow yourself to let your emotional state permeate your work, you can actually do the opposite: something we think of as incredibly measured and analytical, meaning a project, can become something more abstract and suggestive while keeping the same rigor.

SLP

Yeah, I think that the relationship between our emotional state of being and these questions of representation is quite fascinating. And managing that emotional response, the faculties one has to develop, is an important part of the learning curve. I also want to ask you about something else. Did the women who produced and studied these photographs measure the space in between the stars, the white space of the paper?

AS

I honestly don't know. The white space seems left to be. It's a place that stars can move into, but it's not necessarily important

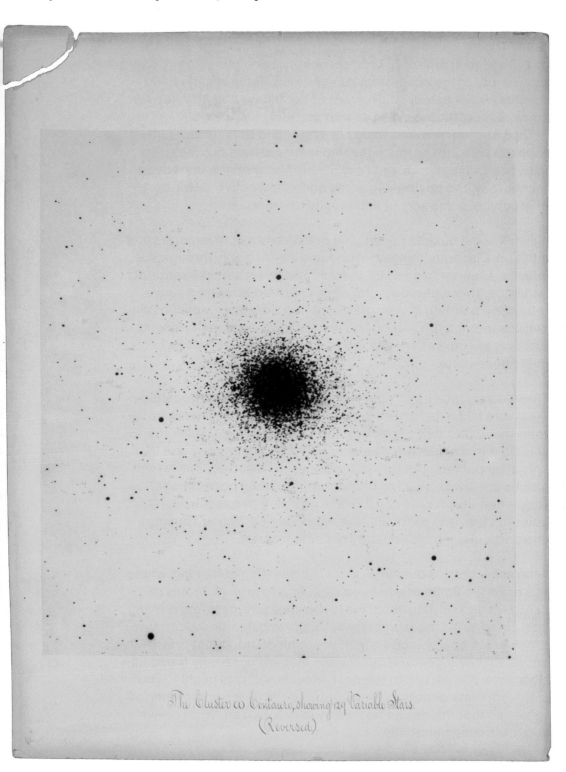

The Cluster ω Centauri, showing 129 Variable Stars.
(Reversed).

other than as a field that is occupied.

SLP

There's one image that says "the new planet Eros, February 16th, 1894." The new planet Eros is a small speck with an arrow next to it. It's kind of amazing. That's probably, I don't know, only one-thousandth of the image, maybe even less. But that's the thing that they want to look at. The rest of the image has no value for some reason: that speck is all that matters.

The space in between things is something that I'm very drawn to all the time. Not so much the things themselves but the space in between the things and how through that space in between things, they end up defining some sort of collective, some sort of grouping, some sort of community of a kind.

AS

This takes me back to my original question about inventories and intuition. Disparate things can become a series only through the intuition to understand them as such, and this is a fundamental act of design. These photographs were captured through a single telescope pointing at a single portion of the changing night sky. Yet, it is through the mental and visual labor of the astronomers that they become a series that's capable of describing more complex phenomena.

SLP

That's a very interesting point. Are they a series just because they were taken one after the other, or does analytical work transform that collection of photographs into a series? I think it's plausible to discuss them initially as a group of images and then, only after pointing out their differences, as a series. Only when graphs are drawn over the photographs do they become a series. Only when they have been linked according to one particular point of view, one particular measure, one particular framing, one particular interest do they become a series.

AS

A big aspect of this design process is a question of framing: where you draw the limits of what you're willing to look at. In this regard, I want to ask you about the role of measurement. You are very interested in the measurability of things and demand a certain precision in how you operate. If we think of individual preferences as purely gestural operations that are not easily transmissible from one person to the next, measurability is pushing you in the opposite direction. Measurability allows a transference of values so that things can be repeated or totalized. What draws you toward measurability?

I think that middle space between individual preferences and universalizing or flattening is precisely where the disciplines of the built environment thrive. And historically, that's where our strength has always been. It's generally a failure when there is a universalizing aspect of any kind, and it's also a failure when there is an attempt to systematically address differences between individuals, because we don't have that subtlety within our disciplines to register them. But we do register differences between institutions, between symbolic representations of different groups of people. Those collectives are the interface between individuals and larger systems. To be clear, I am talking about design disciplines as a whole, not individual designers and their careers. I'm talking about doing this systematically in society over a long duration of time.

This question of measurability and immeasurability addresses our need to communicate, to share, to work with others. And in doing so, there is absolutely a need to be able to quantify and measure in the most precise way possible. The act of design is not an exercise of self-expression. We need to be able to measure everything completely, to the very last thing. At the same time, I think that symbolic representations and meanings that are assigned to space, to form, to materials, to the natural environment are all beyond those measurable quantities. When we look at design from the point of view of the public realm, the idea of representing some collective, some institution, or some group of people is necessarily more than the addition of its parts, in a manner that defies mathematical logic. In these disciplines, one plus one does not equal two. One room plus one room doesn't equal two rooms; it equals a building that represents something of a different quality, whether it's a school or a home or a religious building of some kind.

I see this tension between measurability and immeasurability present in the history of these photographs, especially in their transformation from quantitative to aesthetic objects. How do you view this tension manifesting in design?

This tension is necessary, and it becomes especially interesting in the aesthetic realm. You have to be able to measure things and at the same time accept the immeasurability of the aesthetic resonance that you're working with. You attempt to establish a sensibility that resonates with a lot of people, and in doing so, you need to be able to measure things and be precise. A design needs to be something that defines its own measure in order to become a sensibility and not just something that stays at the level of individual preference.

We can talk about this tension from an aesthetic point of view, from a material point of view, from a spatial, formal, ecological point of view. It exists in all these realms. And I think that this is something that any student of architecture would understand, even if they're not able to verbally articulate it.

I don't think that what I'm saying is that groundbreaking or revolutionary. But I do think that making this tension the core question of a public design project—as simple as it might be— is groundbreaking in some ways. The ambition for the option studio "The Immeasurable Enclosure" is precisely that.[5] On the

This advanced multidisciplinary design studio proposes using immeasurability as the aesthetic and spatial expression of the public realm. Students in this course design one single-space environment using raw phenomena arrested by manufactured structures as the place for a public encounter between communities in conflict.

one hand, it addresses the need to be able to design some type of enclosure that allows communities in conflict to come to-gether for a particular reason. On the other, the aesthetic of that encounter needs to be immeasurable, even though the means to achieve it need to be measurable. It is within this tension, which the students explore aesthetically, materially, formally, and en-vironmentally, that the question of the public realm lies.

fig. 5 The New Planet Eros   *fig.* 6 Meteor Trails, photographed, 1895 and 1898.

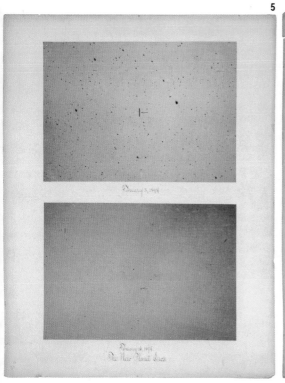

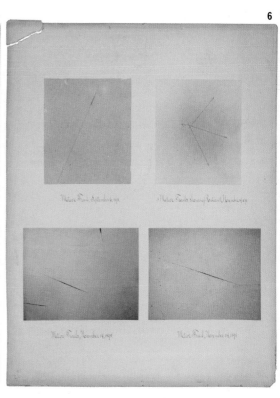

5

6

203

8 EMILY WETTSTEIN is an assistant professor of landscape architecture at the University of Virginia. She is a cofounder of the Seeding Pedagogies Collaborative, where she designs emergent landscape-forward pedagogies. Wettstein was previously a design critic at the Harvard Graduate School of Design, where she taught studios and courses in representation and climate change.

MLA WELCOME PACKAGES are kits that were mailed to 37 incoming Master in Landscape Architecture students when the Harvard Graduate School of Design was completely remote in 2020. Organized by Emily Wettstein, the packages include laser-cut parts for students' first studio site models, large scale plots and prints, scale people cards, isometric and dot notepads, AutoCAD lineweight cheatsheets, an elm tree leaf from Harvard Yard, and a hand-written card.

20 DANIELLE AUBERT is a graphic designer based in Detroit. She is associate professor of graphic design at Wayne State University (WSU) and president of the AAUP-AFT Local 6075, a union made up of the 1,700 academic staff and faculty of WSU. Danielle's publications include *The Detroit Printing Co-op: The Politics and Joy of Printing* and *Thank You For the View, Mr. Mies: Lafayette Park, Detroit.*

The HARVARD UNIVERSITY STRIKE POSTERS are a collection of posters primarily from the 1969 student strike at Harvard University. These posters are silkscreen prints on newsprint, produced by various student printing groups. One group of creators from the design schools at Harvard University and the Massachusetts Institute of Technology operated under the name "Designers for Peace" and worked out of the basement of Harvard's Memorial Hall.

34 THEASTER GATES is an interdisciplinary artist whose work focuses on social practice and installation art. Trained as a potter and urban planner, Gates is the founder of the Rebuild Foundation, a nonprofit cultural organization that aims to uplift under-resourced neighborhoods. He is based in Chicago.

KAREL MILER'S "ACTIONS" are a series of photographs of the artist in semantic translation. Made in Czechoslovakia in the early 1970s, these images were intended to be a form of visual poetry exploring corporality and spatial construction. A Zen practitioner, Miler is concerned with representations of universal and individual forms.

48 SHANNON MATTERN is the Penn Presidential Compact Professor of Media Studies and the History of Art at the University of Pennsylvania. Her research and writing focus on media infrastructures and the intersection of data, art, and design. Previously, she worked in the School of Media Studies and the Department of Anthropology at The New School.

The NANCY GRAVES MAPS showcase the artistic exploration of the sculptor, painter, and printmaker Nancy Graves (1939–1995). Created from the early to mid-1970s, these maps offer a captivating representation of Graves's fascination with natural phenomena. Specifically, she delves into the realm of satellite imagery, incorporating temperature and weather patterns observed on the earth, the moon, and Mars.

64 ERIC ROBSKY HUNTLEY is a geographer and designer whose work centers on "mapping up," a social justice-oriented data science practice that ties forms of oppression to the actors that perpetuate them. They are a lecturer in urban science and planning at the Department of Urban Studies and Planning at the Massachusetts Institute of Technology and chair the Digital Geographies Specialty Group at the American Association of Geographers.

The PAPERS OF HOWARD T. FISHER document the founding of the Harvard Laboratory for Computer Graphics and Spatial Analysis, which Fisher founded in 1965 at the Harvard Graduate School of Design. Created to develop and promote early software technology in computer graphics and analysis, the lab was one of the first to create computer-generated maps.

76 KATE WAGNER is a critic and journalist based in Chicago, Illinois, and Ljubljana, Slovenia. Widely known for her satirical architecture blog *McMansion Hell*, Wagner is *The Nation*'s newest architecture correspondent and a frequent contributor to the *New York Review of Architecture*, *Architectural Review*, *Architect's Newspaper*, *Dwell*, *The Baffler*, *Curbed*, and *The New Republic*. She currently lectures at the University of Chicago's Department of Art History.

THE INDUSTRIAL FILM COLLECTION is an archival collection of 16-mm film shorts from the 1940s to the 1980s gathered and produced by the Harvard Business School with the Harvard University Film Foundation. They vary from instructional and narrative film to advertisement and cover a number of topics, including labor, motion, efficiency, mechanization, industrialization, the relations of management and workers, business policy, and administration.

90 RYAN W. KENNIHAN is an American architect practicing in Dublin. His practice engages critically with building conventions and heritage to deliver deeply thoughtful buildings. Kennihan and his team pull from the immediate context to produce relatively normal forms made impressive by leveraging necessities of structure and functional details, such as rain gutters. The practice was recently featured in *Architectural Review* for an adaptive reuse project of a residential farmhouse.

SITE OF REVERSIBLE DESTINY is a park by artists Arakawa and Madeline Gins in Yoro, Japan, designed with the intention of disrupting the expected in built environments. On the four-acre site, conventional building materials are organized to produce a context of irregularity. The site argues that through radically changing how we engage with the typical, we might outlive the physical artifacts of life that so often survive us.

102 FERNANDA CANALES is a Mexico City-based architect, design critic, and researcher specializing in housing and urban planning. She has authored several books and essays about housing and architecture in Mexico. In 2022, she taught an option studio at the Harvard Graduate School of Design titled "Complete Houses, Designing Non-Fragmented Landscapes of Beds."

The HARVARDEVENS VILLAGE PHOTOGRAPHS document the facilities and community life at Harvardevens Village, Harvard University's post-World War II temporary housing community for married student-veterans at Fort Devens, near Ayer, Massachusetts. The photographs, taken between 1947 and 1949, are amateur snapshots depicting the different aspects of Harvardevens Village and community life.

114 YASMEEN LARI is an architect and humanitarian working to develop Pakistan's built environment through a sustainable grassroots model. As the cofounder and CEO of the Heritage Foundation of Pakistan, she advocates for "barefoot social architecture," a carbon-neutral, traditional, and women-centered approach to housing. In 2023, she was awarded the Royal Gold Medal by the Royal Institute of British Architects.

MIMAR was a quarterly architecture magazine edited by Hasan-Uddin Khan that focused on architecture and the built environment in the developing world. When it was first published in 1981, it was the only journal of its kind. While *Mimar* is no longer in print, its 43 issues are archived online at Archnet.org.

126 MAE-LING LOKKO is a designer, architectural scientist, and educator that re-stories the life cycles of agro-waste and bio-based materials through participatory modes of collaboration and production. Lokko is an assistant professor at the Yale School of Architecture and the founder of Willow Technologies, Ltd., a materials and building technology company based in Accra, Ghana.

The BENIN BRONZES are a collection of four artifacts from the Benin Kingdom held by the Harvard Peabody Museum. This collection includes a beaded coral apron, a bronze plaque of the attendant to the Iyoba (queen mother), a cast bronze altarpiece tableau showing the Iyoba and attendants after her passing, and the idealized bronze head of an Oba (king). These artifacts are part of a larger group of thousands of sculptures, plaques, and objects that were looted from the royal palace during the 1897 Benin Expedition, in today's Edo State, Nigeria.

138 MELANIE BOEHI is a Swiss historian working as a researcher, curator, and editor at the intersection of the humanities, science, and art. Her main research interests are botanical gardens and plants, museums, journalism, and media history. She is particularly fascinated by questions of methodology and form and combines conventional academic research with artistic research, firmly believing that they are equally relevant.

The UNITED FRUIT COMPANY PHOTOGRAPHS document the setup and operations of the US multinational corporation in Central and South America. Housed at the Harvard Business School Library Special Collections, they were made and stored as company records between 1891 and 1962.

152 JEFFREY SHAW is an internationally renowned artist and leading figure in new media art. His work has pioneered the creative use of media such as expanded cinema, immersive visualizations, and augmented reality. Shaw currently serves as chair professor and founding director of the Visualization Research Centre at the Academy of Visual Arts, Hong Kong Baptist University.

MARK ROTHKO'S HARVARD MURALS are a set of five canvas murals installed in 1969 in a penthouse dining room of Harvard University's Holyoke Center. After sustaining sunlight damage, the murals were put in storage in 1979. In 2008, a team at the Harvard Art Museums invented a new way to restore the faded colors of the murals by projecting compensatory light onto the canvases, allowing the murals to be shown in their original colors in a 2014–2015 exhibition.

166 **ÞÓRA PÉTURSDÓTTIR** is an Icelandic archae-ologist and researcher whose work engages with drift material, the afterlife of things, the inter-section of culture and nature, and heritage of the Anthropocene. With a particular interest in the Arctic, she conducts most of her fieldwork in Iceland and northern Norway, and she is an associate professor at the University of Oslo. As editor-in-chief of the journal *Norwegian Archaeological Review*, she is working to advance archaeological knowledge production by ex-ploring different forms of dissemination and communication.

HERBARIA is a 2022 experimental documen-tary by the Argentinian filmmaker and film ar-chivist Leandro Listorti. The film artfully portrays the processes of preserving both plants and film in archives over time. With original and ar-chival content, the film brings together art and science in a meticulous depiction of decay. In September 2022, Listorti joined the Harvard Film Archive for a screening of the film.

178 **STEFANIE HESSLER** is a German curator, writer, and editor. She is the director of the New York-based contemporary art nonprofit Swiss Institute. At large, her work is situated at the juncture between ecology and human society and, more recently, focused on the ocean. Her writing has been published by MIT Press, *Art Review*, and *Art Agenda*, among others.

THE FEEJEE MERMAID is a man-made composite hoax object on display in the exhi-bition *All the World is Here: Harvard's Peabody Museum and the Invention of American An-thropology*. Its long-alleged history and myste-rious origin(s) begin with a Japanese fisher-man, but it is often credited to P.T. Barnum, "America's Greatest Showman."

192 **SERGIO LOPEZ-PINEIRO** is an interdis-ciplinary architect whose work looks at the mutual influence between sociocultural forces and spatial organizations and imagines exist-ing and potential gaps to redefine relations between individual and collective forms of life. Lopez-Pineiro is the author of *A Glossary of Urban Voids* (Jovis, 2020) and *Typologies for Big Words* (ORO Editions, 2023).

The **WILLIAMINA FLEMING ASTRO-NOMICAL PHOTOGRAPHS** are a collection 13 sheets of tan cardstock onto which are glued photographs of Harvard College Obser-vatory buildings; scientific instruments; research stations, including one in Arequipa, Peru; celestial photographs taken with Har-vard astrographs; and records of data analysis, much of it done by women "computers" em-ployed at the Observatory. The cards were used to illustrate a talk about the Observatory and its research.

Editors, Contributors, Designer

EDITORS

I SABEL LEWIS is a GSD Master in Landscape Architecture I student and holds an undergraduate degree in studio art from Reed College. She is from Arlington, Massachusetts.

ADREA P I AZZA is a 2023 graduate of the GSD Master of Architecture I and holds an undergraduate degree in English from Georgetown University. She is from Blue Hill, Maine.

ANDREA SANDELL is a 2023 graduate of the GSD Master of Architecture I and holds undergraduate and graduate degrees in philosophy from Boston College. He is from Tirano, Italy.

Contributors

RA I N CHAN graduated with a Master of Architecture II from the GSD and a bachelor of architecture from the Cooper Union. He currently runs an exhibition design practice and serves as an adjunct assistant professor at Pratt Institute and the New York Institute of Technology. He is from Hong Kong.

SOPH I E WESTON CH I EN is a GSD Master in Landscape Architecture and Master in Urban Planning student and previously studied at the Rhode Island School of Design, where she received a bachelor of architecture and a bachelor of fine arts. She is from Catawba, Cheraw, and Sugaree land (Charlotte, North Carolina).

L I Z CORMACK is a 2023 graduate of the GSD Master in Urban Planning. She previously studied communication design at Emerson College and now works as an associate urban planner at Agency Landscape + Planning in Cambridge, Massachusetts. She grew up in Seoul, Warsaw, Paris, and Northern Virginia.

SYEDA A I MEN FAT I MA is a spatial designer passionate about climate justice and the built environment. She completed the GSD Master of Architecture in Urban Design and a bachelor of architecture at Beaconhouse National University. She is from Lahore, Pakistan.

EM I LY HSEE is a GSD Master of Architecture I student and holds an undergraduate degree in architecture from Yale University. She is from Chicago, Illinois.

ARET I KOTSON I is an interdisciplinary researcher and licensed architectural engineer from Chania, Greece. She completed the GSD Master in Design Studies and is now a research associate at the GSD and an adjunct professor at Wentworth Institute of Technology.

JENN I FER L I holds a Master of Architecture II from the GSD and a bachelor of architecture from California Polytechnic State University. She chaired both the Womxn in Design and GSD National Organization of Minority Architecture Students organizations during her thesis year. Hailing from the San Francisco Bay Area, Jen is currently a design associate at Alloy Development and a freelance writer based in Brooklyn.

SUMAYYAH SÚNMÁDÉ RAJ I is a designer and storyteller passionate about community design and craftsmanship in communities of color. She is a 2023 graduate of the GSD Master of Architecture I and has a bachelor of science in architecture and environmental design from Morgan State University. She is from Lagos, Nigeria.

JUL I A SPACKMAN is a GSD Master of Architecture I student and holds an undergraduate degree in architecture from the College of Environmental Design at the University of California, Berkeley. She is from Los Angeles, California.

RAPHAELE TAYVAH is a 2023 graduate of the GSD Master in Landscape Architecture and holds an undergraduate degree from Smith College, where they studied art history and museums and translation studies. They are from New York City and Portland, Oregon.

COCO TIN completed the GSD Master in Design Studies and a bachelor of architecture with a minor in art history at Cornell University. She is from Hong Kong and is currently a strategist at 2x4 in New York City.

AUDREY WATKINS a designer and musician from Kenton, Ohio. She is a Master of Architecture I student at the GSD and a graduate of the Columbia University and Juilliard School dual program.

Designer

TEAM MAO develops creative direction and visual narratives for institutions, brands, and individuals. Based in Berlin, Team Mao collaborates internationally, with work ranging from publications, exhibitions, branding, and campaign design to independent projects and design education. The Team Mao design approach focuses on exploring visual aesthetics in a social context.

Image Credits

The editors of *Pairs* are grateful for all permissions to reproduce copyrighted material in this issue. Every effort has been made to trace the ownership of copyrighted material and to secure proper credits and permissions from the appropriate copyright holders. In the event of any omission or oversight, please contact the editorial team and all necessary corrections will be made in future printings.

Emily Wettstein & MLA Welcome Packages
Fig. 1 - 4: Photographs and illustration courtesy of Emily Wettstein.

Danielle Aubert & Harvard Strike Posters
Fig. 1: HUA 969.100.2 (93). Harvard University Archives.
Fig. 2: HUA 969.100.2 (50). Harvard University Archives.
Fig. 3: Bibliothèque nationale de France
Fig. 4: HUA 969.100.2 (116). Harvard University Archives.
Fig. 5: HUA 969.100.2 (106). Harvard University Archives
Fig. 6: HUA 969.100.2 (38). Harvard University Archives.
Fig. 7: HUA 969.100.2 (161). Harvard University Archives.

Theaster Gates & Karel Miler's "Actions"
Fig. 1: *Limits*, Karel Miler, 1973.
Fig. 2: *Either* - or, Karel Miler, 1972.
Fig. 3: *Grating*, Karel Miler, 1974.
Fig. 4: *Identification*, Karel Miler, 1973.

Shannon Mattern & Nancy Graves Maps
Fig. 1: Edition printed by David Keister; Nancy Graves; Landfall Press Inc.; Published by Carl Solway Gallery, *Riphaeus Mountains Region of the Moon*, Harvard Art Museums/Fogg Museum, Gift of Anne MacDougall and Gil Einstein in honor of Marjorie B. Cohn, © Nancy Graves Foundation / Artists Rights Society (ARS), New York, Photo: President and Fellows of Harvard College, M26547.10
Fig. 2: Nancy Graves; Edition printed by Jerry Raidiger; Landfall Press Inc.; Published by Carl Solway Gallery, *Part of Sabine D. Region, Southwest Mare Tranquilitatis*, Harvard Art Museums/Fogg Museum, Gift of Anne MacDougall and Gil Einstein in honor of Marjorie B. Cohn, © Nancy Graves Foundation / Artists Rights Society (ARS), New York, Photo: President and Fellows of Harvard College, M26547.1
Fig. 3: Edition printed by David Keister; Nancy Graves; Landfall Press Inc.; Published by Carl Solway Gallery, *Fra Mauro Region of the Moon*, Harvard Art Museums/Fogg Museum, Gift of Anne MacDougall and Gil Einstein in honor of Marjorie B. Cohn, © Nancy Graves Foundation / Artists Rights Society (ARS), New York, Photo: President and Fellows of Harvard College, M26547.2
Fig. 4: Edition printed by Jerry Raidiger; Nancy Graves; Landfall Press Inc.; Published by Carl Solway Gallery, *Julius Caesar Quadrangle of the Moon*, Harvard Art Museums/Fogg Museum, Gift of Anne MacDougall and Gil Einstein in honor of Marjorie B. Cohn, © Nancy Graves Foundation / Artists Rights Society (ARS), New York, Photo: President and Fellows of Harvard College, M26547.4
Fig. 5: Edition printed by David Keister; Nancy Graves; Landfall Press Inc.; Published by Carl Solway Gallery, *Montes Apenninus Region of the Moon*, Harvard Art Museums/Fogg Museum, Gift of Anne MacDougall and Gil Einstein in honor of Marjorie B. Cohn, © Nancy Graves Foundation / Artists Rights Society (ARS), New York, Photo: President and Fellows of Harvard College, M26547.5
Fig. 6: Nancy Graves; Edition printed by David Keister; Landfall Press Inc.; Published by Carl Solway Gallery, *Maskelyne DA Region of the Moon*, Harvard Art Museums/Fogg Museum, Gift of Anne MacDougall and Gil Einstein in honor of Marjorie B. Cohn, © Nancy Graves Foundation / Artists Rights Society (ARS), New York, Photo: President and Fellows of Harvard College, M26547.6

Eric Robsky Huntley & Papers of Howard T. Fisher
Fig. 1 - 5: Courtesy of the Harvard University Archives.

Kate Wagner & The Industrial Film Collection
Fig. 1 - 10: The Industrial Film Collection. Part of the Baker Library Special Collections and Archives, Harvard Business School Repository. The films in this series were either purchased or acquired by the Graduate School of Business Administration.

Ryan W. Kennihan & Site of Reversible Destiny
Fig. 1 - 9: Courtesy of the Harvard University Graduate School of Design, Frances Loeb Library Visual Collections, © 2005, John Beardsley.

Fernanda Canales & Harvardevens Photographs
Fig. 1: HUF 442.547 Box 1, Folder 2 (1). Harvard University Archives
Fig. 2: HUF 442.547 Box 1, Folder 16 (30). Harvard University Archives.

Colophon

EDITORS
Isabel Lewis
Adrea Piazza
Andrea Sandell

CONTRIBUTORS
Rain Chan
Sophie Weston Chien
Liz Cormack
Syeda Aimen Fatima
Emily Hsee
Areti Kotsoni
Jennifer Li
Sumayyah Súnmádé Raji
Julia Spackman
Raphaele Tayvah
CoCo Tin
Audrey Watkins

GRAPHIC DESIGN
Team Mao, Berlin:
Siyu Mao, Robyn Steffen

PRINTING
Grafiche Veneziane Società
Cooperative

COPYEDITING
Arts Editing Services: Tyler
Considine, Liz Janoff

ADVISORS
Ken Stewart, Marielle Suba,
Sarah M. Whiting, Inés
Zalduendo

THANKS
Issue 04 of *Pairs* would not
have been possible without
the generosity and support
of Francesca Bewer, Sarah
Clunis, Ebube Dike, James
Grant, Olivia Howard, Leonard
Palmer, Maleah Piazza,
Heebah Raji, Eric Schwartz,
and Kyle Winston.

PAIRS
Pairs was founded in 2019
by students Nicolás Delgado
Álcega, Vladimir Gintoff, and
Kimberley Huggins with the
support of Dean Sarah M.
Whiting and the Harvard
University Graduate School
of Design.

TYPEFACES
Oracle
Oracle Triple

PAPER
Splendorlux

COVER IMAGE
Herbaria, 2022, 1:15:13.

1,000 copies printed and
bound in Venice, Italy, September 2023

ISBN 978-1-934510-92-6